# Praise for
# *The Deep End of Hope* ... *Hurricane H*...

If you want to experience the Helene catastrophe at ground level, let me recommend Emma Churchman's *The Deep End of Hope in the Wake of Hurricane Helene*. She stitches together each day and many of the people in tiny Gerton, North Carolina. She shows how everyone went into survival mode and how many regular neighbors became heroes. This book is full of heartfelt stories and hope in the midst of devastation.

John Ager (D)
Former Representative, North Carolina House

Hurricane Helene was a devastating event for Western North Carolina and throughout the Southeast. This book is a must-read for politicians and legislators, as well as disaster relief organizations and business leaders, to understand the true impact of living through such a horrendous event and the following long-term recovery implications. The stories of resilience and transformation in this small rural Appalachian community will pull at your heartstrings.

Timothy Moffitt (R)
State Senator, District 48: Henderson, Polk,
and Rutherford Counties, North Carolina

This is the best book I have read this year and in my lifetime. Even having been in the area of destruction, I did not realize the true damage in the surrounding communities. So many were experiencing trauma, but I was focused on what was lost. This book and this author will heal so many including those who did not even realize they needed healing. Please take this journey and experience the immediate aftermath of the hurricane. Then, ask yourself, what can I do to ensure those needing help and support have that throughout the very *long* road of recovery to their uncertain future?

Pamela Prince-Eason<br>
President & CEO, Women's Business<br>
Enterprise National Council

# THE DEEP END OF HOPE

## IN THE WAKE OF HURRICANE HELENE

**40** DAYS AND NIGHTS OF SURVIVAL AND TRANSFORMATION

EMMA M. CHURCHMAN, MDIV

Copyright © 2025 by Emma M. Churchman, MDIV

*The Deep End of Hope in the Wake of Hurricane Helene:*
*40 Days and Nights of Survival and Transformation*

All rights reserved.

No part of this work may be used or reproduced, transmitted, stored, or used in any form or by any means graphic, electronic, or mechanical, including but not limited to photocopying, recording, scanning, digitizing, taping, Web distribution, information networks or information storage and retrieval systems, or in any manner whatsoever without prior written permission from the publisher.

In this world of digital information and rapidly changing technology, some citations do not provide exact page numbers or credit the original source. We regret any errors which are a result of the ease with which we consume information.

The information in this book is a truthful recollection of actual events in the author's life. The names and identifying characteristics of individuals and places may have been changed to maintain anonymity.

This book deals with sensitive topics including suicide, mental health challenges, and trauma. The content may be emotionally challenging. The author aims to handle these topics with care while exploring themes of resilience, healing and hope.

Cover Photo Credit: Jeff Boudreaux, Julia Pierce, Tarin Truluck
Author Photo Credit: Jeff Boudreaux

An Imprint for GracePoint Publishing (www.GracePointPublishing.com)
GracePoint Matrix, LLC
624 S. Cascade Ave, Suite 201, Colorado Springs, CO 80903
www.GracePointMatrix.com   Email: Admin@GracePointMatrix.com
SAN # 991-6032

ISBN: (Paperback) 978-1-966346-10-4
eISBN: 978-1-966346-11-1

Books may be purchased for educational, business, or sales promotional use.
For bulk order requests and price schedule contact:
Orders@GracePointPublishing.com

## Dedication

To my husband, Jeff, without whose help this book would not be possible: There is no one I'd rather live through an apocalypse with.

# TABLE OF CONTENTS

**FOREWORD** ........................................................................... **XI**

**PREFACE** ............................................................................. **XV**

**INTRODUCTION** ..................................................................... 1

### PART 1: RESCUE

Day 1—9/27/24 ........................................................................ 9
Day 2—9/28/24 ...................................................................... 13
Day 3—9/29/24 ...................................................................... 21
Day 4 of the Apocalypse—9/30/24 ................................................ 29
Day 5 of the Apocalypse ........................................................... 33
Day 6 of the Apocalypse ........................................................... 37
Day 7 of the Apocalypse Gerton, NC, Pop. 300 ................................. 47
Day 8 of the Apocalypse Gerton, NC, Pop. 300 301 ............................ 53
Day 9 of the Apocalypse Gerton, NC, Pop. 301 ................................. 61
Day 10 of the Apocalypse Gerton, NC, Pop. 301 ............................... 65
Reflections on Trauma in the Rescue Phase .................................... 71

### PART 2: RECOVERY

Day 11 of the Apocalypse Gerton, NC, Pop. 301 ............................... 77
Day 12 of the Apocalypse Ground Zero, Gerton, NC, Pop. 301 ............... 85
Day 13 of the Apocalypse Ground Zero, Gerton, NC, Pop. 301 ............... 89
Day 14 of the Apocalypse Ground Zero, Gerton, NC, Pop. 301 ............... 93
Day 15 of the Apocalypse Ground Zero, Gerton, NC, Pop. 301 ............... 97
Day 16 of the Apocalypse Ground Zero, Gerton, NC, Pop. 301 ............. 101
Day 17 of the Apocalypse Ground Zero, Gerton, NC, Pop. 301 ............. 105
Day 18 of the Apocalypse Ground Zero, Gerton, NC, Pop. 301 ............. 109
Day 19 of the Apocalypse Ground Zero, Gerton, NC, Pop. 301 ............. 113
Day 20 of the Apocalypse Ground Zero, Gerton, NC, Pop. 301 ............. 117
Day 21 of the Apocalypse Ground Zero, Gerton, NC, Pop. 301 ............. 121

Day 22 of the Apocalypse Ground Zero, Gerton, NC, Pop. 301 ............. 127
Reflections on Trauma in the Recovery Phase ................................... 131

### PART 3: RECONSTRUCTION

Day 23 of the Apocalypse Ground Zero, Gerton, NC, Pop. 301 ............. 137
Day 24 of the Apocalypse Ground Zero, Gerton, NC, Pop. 301 ............. 141
Day 25 of the Apocalypse Ground Zero, Gerton, NC, Pop. 301 ............. 145
Day 26 of the Apocalypse Ground Zero, Gerton, NC, Pop. 301 ............. 151
Day 27 of the Apocalypse Ground Zero, Gerton, NC, Pop. 301 ............. 157
Day 28 of the Apocalypse Ground Zero, Gerton, NC, Pop. 301 ............. 161
Day 29 of the Apocalypse Ground Zero, Gerton, NC, Pop. 301 ............. 165
Day 30 of the Apocalypse Ground Zero, Gerton, NC, Pop. 301 ............. 173
Day 31 of the Apocalypse Ground Zero, Gerton, NC, Pop. 301 ............. 177
Day 32 of the Apocalypse Ground Zero, Gerton, NC, Pop. 301 ............. 181
Reflections on Trauma in the Reconstruction Phase .......................... 185

### PART 4: EVOLUTION

Day 33 of the Apocalypse Ground Zero, Gerton, NC, Pop. 301 ............. 193
Day 34 of the Apocalypse Ground Zero, Gerton, NC, Pop. 301 ............. 195
Day 35 of the Apocalypse Ground Zero, Gerton, NC, Pop. 301 ............. 199
Day 36 of the Apocalypse Ground Zero, Gerton, NC, Pop. 301 ............. 203
Day 37 of the Apocalypse Ground Zero, Gerton, NC, Pop. 301 ............. 207
Day 38 of the Apocalypse Ground Zero, Gerton, NC, Pop. 301 ............. 211
Day 39 of the Apocalypse Ground Zero, Gerton, NC, Pop. 301 ............. 213
Day 40 of the Apocalypse Ground Zero, Gerton, NC, Pop. 301 ............. 215
Reflections on Trauma in the Evolution Phase .................................. 219

**EPILOGUE** ........................................................................................ **223**

**NEXT STEPS** .................................................................................... **225**

Your Next Steps ............................................................................... 227
Trauma Recovery in Real Time Self-led Online Course ................... 228
Keynote Speaker .............................................................................. 230

**ACKNOWLEDGMENTS** .................................................................... **233**

**ABOUT THE AUTHOR** ...................................................................... **235**

*This is precisely the time when artists go to work. There is no time for despair, no place for self-pity, no need for silence, no room for fear. We speak, we write, we do language. That is how civilizations heal.*

*I know the world is bruised and bleeding, and though it is important not to ignore its pain, it is also critical to refuse to succumb to its malevolence. Like failure, chaos contains information that can lead to knowledge—even wisdom. Like Art.*

—Toni Morrison

# FOREWORD

In my twenty-one years as executive director of Mennonite Disaster Service (MDS), Emma Churchman's account of the aftermath of Hurricane Helene is one of the most gripping post-disaster stories I have ever read. As you absorb the story of how she and her husband Jeff coped not only with their own trauma but also helped others, you will get a sense of the sadness, fear, gratitude, and healing that Emma, Jeff, and their community of Gerton, North Carolina, experienced.

Gerton, population 301 people, is quite close to Fairview (southeast of Asheville), where MDS set up its base camp on the property of longtime MDS volunteer, Phil Troyer. Because MDS began its response within a week after Helene hit, we got to know Emma—and Gerton—quite early on.

The communities of Gerton and Bat Cave are seen as the backwater part of the comparatively wealthy Henderson County. At the time this book is being printed, there are many people who still need financial and logistical help rebuilding homes, private roads, and bridges, along with clearing their properties of storm debris. To date, counties and the Federal Emergency Management Agency (FEMA) are struggling to provide assistance. Families are being turned down every day by their insurance companies and are left to figure out what to do with their uninhabitable homes.

Gerton, Western North Carolina, and other parts of the Southeast affected by Helene are on a challenging path to long-term recovery.

There is a math equation called the "principle of 10s" that disaster organizations use to determine how long recovery will take following a catastrophic event. The calculation works like this: If the rescue (saving lives and ensuring public safety and well-being) lasts ten days, then relief (ensuring road access for emergencies and removing trees from homes) takes about one hundred days, and recovery (rehoming people, longer term solutions for food and water, kids going back to school, etc.) requires about 1000 days... or three years. There are many different factors that affect this principle. For example, if there is an existing long-term recovery group involved, or previous experience, this may shorten the time frame exponentially.

In areas affected by Hurricane Helene, it will take a minimum of ten years—and most likely decades—to fully recover from this natural disaster. Thousands of people will continue to live in an apocalyptic world for years to come.

This book contains technical information about disasters: how climate change may affect weather events, how disaster response is divided into stages, and a day-to-day account of what it's like to be cut off from the world, not sure if or when water and food will run out, all while physically, mentally, emotionally, and spiritually traumatized.

Emma's book is primarily about the emergency response and early phase of disaster—the phase in which many people experience the trauma from which they will spend months or even years recovering.

Shining through a lot of dark realities is the light of love Emma has for her neighbors. She processes her experience through a lens of love: love for people who have helped Gerton and love for the land and its capacity to heal.

This is, as she writes, "a fierce love," the kind of love that is the backbone of disaster recovery, the kind of love we need when everything is uncertain, a godly kind of love. I think of Psalm 46:1: "God is our refuge and strength, a very present help in trouble."

Emma has been a very present help to her community, as I have seen so many MDS volunteers strive to be while they help those most in need. As Emma wrote: "Most of us are doing what we can to positively impact others, regardless of what's going on for us personally."

When we work to get someone back home or back to normal after a disaster, we sometimes wonder: *What is normal, anyway?* Emma shows us through her heartfelt story that the process is as important as the outcome.

I loved reading about how Emma is part of the Anabaptist community. She is a practicing Quaker and a national speaker. She became a Quaker minister twenty years ago and then a trauma chaplain a dozen years ago. As you will read, she got a kick out of introducing herself to MDS as a Quaker minister. "Finally, I am an Anabaptist among Anabaptists, not a common occurrence in this part of the country," she writes.

On day seven in the wake of Helene, MDS volunteers showed up in Gerton to help clean up.

A portion of the proceeds of this book will go to Mennonite Disaster Service—because we were one of the first groups in Gerton helping with the devastation.

MDS is committed to the long-term recovery from this event. We have been tasked by FEMA to help reconstruct 5,000 private bridges in the region impacted by Helene. We expect to have volunteers in Western North Carolina for at least the next two years, helping with recovery efforts.

May God bless Gerton. And may God bless the long-term recovery process for everyone impacted by Hurricane Helene.

Kevin King<br>
Executive Director<br>
Mennonite Disaster Service

# PREFACE

I was born into trauma. Generations of it paved an exquisite path for my arrival fifty years ago.

I was raised by a depressive, alcoholic father and a suicidal mother with an extreme case of multiple personality disorder. Our home was filled with violence and emotional betrayal.

Our father died by suicide when I was twenty-four and my brothers were twenty-two, sixteen, and twelve. They were well on their way to a life of alcohol and drug addiction in attempts to cope with the reality of our family. After years of struggle, they each ended their lives too. I chose another path. I chose to heal and transform my trauma.

I don't know why I chose this path. Perhaps it was adolescent rebellion. More realistically, it was the only way I found to survive in a family that didn't want to live.

My coping mechanism as a child was to become the person others needed me to be—who my parents and brothers needed.

My becoming a Quaker minister twenty years ago, and then a trauma chaplain a dozen years ago, was born from that coping mechanism, but also from a deep belief that there is a greater way to live in this world.

Love is that way. Love is what allows for healing and transformation.

It is possible to attend to your own trauma and still help others. There is always a way through. That's what Love shows us and teaches us.

On September 26, 2024, when Hurricane Helene devastated our tiny community of Gerton (population 300), in Western North Carolina, a small voice inside of me told me to show up in Love for my community.

I became their trauma chaplain.

This book is based on daily Facebook posts I shared during the first forty days following the hurricane[1] as a way to let people know what was going on. It is the daily journey of our tiny community in the wake of a hurricane and my own experience of processing and attending to the trauma from this extreme geological event, the likes of which haven't been seen since the formation of Earth itself, since the appearance of the oceans or early life forms, since the formation of supercontinents like Pangaea, or since the event that wiped out dinosaurs.

This book is also a love letter to the small communities of rural Appalachia and a call to action for our nation to do better with honoring and supporting these incredibly resilient people.

It is also a wake-up call. Many scientists tell us climate change will increase the frequency and severity of natural disasters like ours. Greenpeace International and World Weather Attribution stated that climate change induced by fossil fuel warming caused the extreme weather patterns and influenced the severity of Helene.

---

[1] By definition, hurricanes start as disturbances when clouds, heavy with evaporated warm water become organized over large bodies of water. These bands of thunderstorms, if organized, become disturbances, but if they grow, they become depressions. If the system remains organized and increases in wind speed to 74 mph, they are named hurricanes. Most hurricanes lose speed as they approach landfall and begin to decay. These leftover bands of thunderstorms with heavy rain and wind gusts from the once-organized hurricane are what devastated our area.

## The Deep End of Hope in the Wake of Hurricane Helene

I did find one source that indicated Helene was *not* caused by climate change. The Thomas Jefferson Institute for Public Policy stated that Hurricane Helene was not worse than other storm events, like the Great Flood of 1916, or other storms from decades or even a century ago. According to this institute, "as more people move to and build more buildings and parking lots in coastal surge zones and 100-year flood plains, creating more impermeable surfaces and structures to be wiped out, the flooding will just get worse."[2]

Just during the writing of this book, two other major disasters struck. Milton, a category 3 hurricane, made landfall in Florida on October 9th, taking thirty-five lives (according to multiple news sources).[3] World Weather Attribution also claimed that climate change enhanced the conditions of Milton, with more intense rainfall totals and wind speeds. Elevated ocean temperatures encouraged more humidity to form. In this case, the ocean temperature at Milton's birth was 87 degrees Fahrenheit, about two degrees warmer than normal.[4]

According to many news sources, catastrophic flash flooding on October 29th, in Valencia, Spain, claimed 217 lives. The flood was one of the deadliest weather events in modern Spanish history, dumping a year's worth of rain in eight hours, and devastating sixty-nine localities. Climate scientists and meteorologists indicated the immediate cause of the flooding is called a cutoff low, a lower-pressure storm system that came from a stalled jet stream and dumped an historic amount of rain. This was combined with the unusually high temperature of the Mediterranean Sea. According to Mercator Ocean

---

[2] https://www.thomasjeffersoninst.org/no-rtd-hurricane-helene-not-proof-of-climate-change/

[3] Facts and numbers regarding the climate, the ocean, and recent disasters are being updated regularly on news and information sources. We have made every attempt to validate and verify the figures detailed herein.

[4] https://www.post-journal.com/news/top-stories/2024/10/heres-what-has-made-hurricane-milton-so-fierce-and-unusual/

International, the Mediterranean Sea had its warmest surface temperature on record in mid-August 2024, at 83.25 degrees Fahrenheit. Warmer ocean water allows for more humidity.

Regardless of the cause, it is time for all of us to be prepared for unprecedented events. We no longer have the luxury of remaining observers, grateful that it didn't happen to us. Our opportunity lies in not only being prepared as best we can, but also in learning how to process trauma as we are going through it.

# INTRODUCTION

This past spring, our community center had a showing of an hour-long documentary about the Great Flood of 1916. Up until Helene, it was the flood by which all other floods were measured here in Western North Carolina. It was considered a one-in-one-thousand-year event. The locals call it the Great Flood for that reason.

The Great Flood caused the most destruction and devastation to date in our part of North Carolina, close to $500 million in today's currency.

The Great Flood was the result of two tropical storms converging here in the mountains. The first came up from the Gulf of Mexico via Alabama on July 5th as a category 3 hurricane (prior to the trend of naming such storms). That storm reached the mountains by July 7th and then stalled, dumping water for seven days straight. By the end, the rivers were at flood stage.

A second storm arrived on July 14th, from the Atlantic via Charleston, South Carolina, with torrential rains that heaped twenty-two inches of rainfall in twenty-four hours on the mountains.

Floodwaters still rose even after the rains stopped on July 16th because the water had nowhere to go. The French Broad River, which runs through Asheville, expanded from a maximum width of 381 feet to nearly 1,500 feet, or a third of a mile. The water reached twenty-one feet in height during the second storm, which is seventeen feet *above* flood stage. With Helene, the water reached thirty-one feet.

To put that in perspective, the average height of a two-story house is twenty-five feet.

Both times, a biblical amount of rain was dumped in too short an amount of time.

During the Great Flood of 1916, dams burst, bridges were demolished, and Asheville's power plant was destroyed. Railroad tracks were suspended sixty feet in the air when the structure beneath them was ripped away by the ferocity of the waters.

The rivers rose so quickly, people had to abandon cars and climb trees to save themselves. Eighty people were officially declared dead, although many suspect the number was much higher. Just like with Helene, mudslides wiped out entire families.

My husband Jeff and I knew understanding the Great Flood was important, but we had a schedule conflict and were unable to attend the documentary showing. We still wanted to know what had happened, so we could be sure to prevent it from happening to us.

Someone from the community center offered to lend us the documentary videotape. Our friend Jen gave us her VCR so we could watch it, but the VCR sat in the back seat of Jeff's truck for weeks, and for whatever reason we never got the tape.

Our logical minds kicked into gear. *Surely we couldn't be affected by this kind of flooding because we live so far up a mountain. Surely the infrastructure of our area had changed so dramatically in the past 108 years that our rivers could not flood now.*

On some level we believed this documentary would give us evidence that another great flood couldn't or *wouldn't* happen to us. Watching it would make us immune.

Jeff was able to get a book about the Great Flood, and yet still we couldn't quite envision the actual effects of flooding in the mountains.

## The Deep End of Hope in the Wake of Hurricane Helene

Both of us come from sea level or below—Jeff from New Orleans and me, Washington, DC—so the idea of mountains collapsing is incomprehensible to us.

As the months passed, the Great Flood became a niggling thought in the recesses of our minds; it was something that we knew we needed to pay attention to, but never quite found a way to.

Our intuition always knows. *How did our community center happen to show this documentary only four months before Helene hit? Why did Jeff and I get the nudge to pay attention?*

Most intuitive guidance is illogical. It shows up as a small whisper, or a fleeting thought—easily dismissed because it's not rational, like our brains like. It's the small voice telling us to take a different route than the one we normally take to work, and then later that day we learn of a fatal accident on our normal route. Often, it's inconvenient or strange. The more we follow it, though, the more we are divinely guided and protected. Those little niggling thoughts matter. Don't take that normal route when something inside says to take a longer path.

On Day 4, when I hiked down the mountain and saw the devastation from Hurricane Helene for myself, I immediately thought about the people in 1916 and their grandchildren and great-grandchildren, many of whom still live on this mountain. I imagined the fear they must have felt when the rain was pounding down and the wind was whipping by. It reminded me that their very genetic makeup includes the Great Flood of 1916.

In my work as trauma chaplain, families who have been here for generations shared with me the stories of their grandparents and great-grandparents during the Great Flood. Such stories include a baby ripped from her mother's arms and washed away by the water; older family members who couldn't get to higher ground quickly enough, and who perished; the heartache and struggles of starting over with nothing. This was not an intended legacy for these families. Each generation wants for those who come after them to escape the hardships and sufferings they experienced.

But then it happened to them, too.

This land carries the imprint of the Great Flood as well: It remembers how the water moved then. Now it also carries the memory of Helene. The land never forgets.

What we choose to pay attention to matters.

In the wake of Hurricane Helene, the devastation is now being considered a severe geological event, due to nearly 2,000 landslides and entire towns being wiped out. The overarching statistics from PBS for this event in North Carolina alone are mind-blowing:

- 1,893 landslides
- 126,000 damaged homes
- 1,000 damaged public bridges and culverts
- 6,000 miles of road damage
- 160 damaged water and sewage systems
- $53 billion in damages

Floodwaters raced through valleys and gorges, causing this massive devastation. Our rugged topography compounded the wind and rain's destructive power. Ridges acted like the walls to a funnel, allowing winds to concentrate and strengthen. Our region's elevation, ranging from 2,000 feet to 6,600 feet above sea level, also meant winds were far more intense than they might have been closer to the coast, reaching 40-90 mph.

Helene caused catastrophic damage across a fifth of the region's million-acre, federally protected forests, according to the North Carolina Forest Service. Because many trees were rooted in soil that is relatively shallow, the intense waters devastated the forests, causing millions of trees to be lost in the wake of Helene. It will take decades for the forests to grow back to their pre-Helene state.

Helene also upended the ecology and aquatic habitats of Western North Carolina. The long-term effects of this keep rolling in.

The hurricane also destroyed crops and farms in all affected states. Early estimates from Florida's Department of Agriculture and Consumer Services indicate between $500 million and $800 million in crop and farm infrastructure losses in Florida alone. North Carolina damage assessments have not been made public, as of this writing.

A hydrologist, using National Oceanic and Atmospheric Administration (NOAA) data, determined Helene to be a 30,000-year storm event, marking it as one of the most significant storm events in US history. In comparison, Hurricane Katrina was a 400-year event.

This book focuses on the impact of Hurricane Helene in our small community and is organized into four parts: Rescue, Recovery, Reconstruction, and Evolution. Each part is a phase of addressing devastation and trauma—physically, mentally, emotionally and spiritually. Part 1: Rescue, represents the first phase following a disaster: of shock and disbelief and of trying to assess what has happened. In Part 2: Recovery, the initial assessment is completed, and the shock has worn off. The focus becomes triaging damage and making sense of it—physically, emotionally, mentally and spiritually. In Part 3: Reconstruction, the object becomes reconstructing ourselves and our surroundings. In the final part, Part 4: Evolution, the spotlight is on where we go from here: in our healing, transformation, and new ways of living and operating.

I have done my best to create a distinction between the different physical, mental, emotional, and spiritual responses in each phase. However, please note that each phase can take much longer than just a week or ten days to address.

# PART 1
# RESCUE

## Day 1—9/27/24

Before Hurricane Helene even arrived in full force, our area had already sustained twenty-one inches of rainfall, breaking records dating back to the Great Flood of 1916. The rain caused our creeks and rivers to overflow.

We went into Asheville on Wednesday afternoon before the hurricane-level rains showed up, like we always do: working out at the gym, running errands, and eating out. Before leaving our mountain, we stopped at Bearwallow Provision Company, our general store here in Gerton, and talked with a few of our neighbors, jokingly asking each other if everyone had stocked up enough on water, toilet paper, bread, and milk.

We'd seen some flooding before in Asheville, especially in Biltmore Village, which is right next to the French Broad River, and knew that probably people would panic. And when people panic with any upcoming potential crisis, they somehow think that water, toilet paper, bread, and milk will give them comfort.

The torrential rain began falling while we were eating dinner. We came home to heavy rain pelting against the windows and doors. Jeff and I rushed inside, drenched from darting just the few feet between the car and our laundry room door. We had to drag our dogs, Winston and Leroy (two miniature dachshunds who do *not* appreciate inclement weather), outside to pee. Jeff turned on the TV, to drown out the steady pelting of raindrops splattering against our house.

There have been many hurricane warnings during the twelve years I've lived in this area. But we're in the mountains of Western North Carolina, 300 miles in from the coast. By the time anything reaches us, most hurricanes have turned into heavy rain or nothing.

Asheville is nestled between mountains. In fact, there is a ring of mountains surrounding Asheville, and people here believe that we are protected by this ancient ring. Previous hurricanes had thrown themselves against these mountains and just whimpered and died.

This has been a steady mantra since I moved here: "The mountains always protect us." When I was their chaplain, my hospice patients in the "hollers" in Madison County, NC, would continually remind me of this. This is how they made sense of the world: They were divinely safeguarded by God and the mountains. The mountains were perfectly designed to look after and provide for us with shelter, food, and water.

Until Helene hit.

Our town of Gerton sits in the northernmost part of the Hickory Nut Gorge. Below us lie Bat Cave, Chimney Rock, and Lake Lure, all connected in a row by the same fourteen-mile-long highway, that goes straight down the cross-shaped gorge.

Our four little communities are also tied together by an interconnected system of streams, creeks, and rivers that get progressively larger as they run down the Gorge. This is what can allow for massive flooding. The mountains funnel rain runoff down our narrow gorge. The streams, creeks, and Rocky Broad River all converge, creating a massive volume of water that then streams through Bat Cave, Chimney Rock, and into Lake Lure.

By 7:00 a.m. this morning, the wind was at a violent 75 miles an hour, still strong enough to be considered a hurricane. Jeff, our dogs, and I are huddled in our king-sized bed in our bedroom. The bedroom

## The Deep End of Hope in the Wake of Hurricane Helene

overlooks our backyard via French doors, which lead out to our back deck. Jeff is trying to make us invisible to harm by insisting we keep the shades down on the doors, not that we can see much beyond the doors anyway. Fall has arrived, and leaves are beginning to cover the ground. Between the wind, rain, and fallen leaves, all visibility is gone.

But we can still hear everything: the rain, slapping against the house; trees cracking and falling. Thud. Crack. Slap. That continues for another five hours, while ten more inches of rain lands on an already saturated earth.

A record thirty-one inches of rain falls in the span of forty hours.

When the rain finally stops completely shortly before noon, Jeff and I venture outside to assess damage. We have one big tree down on our back slope. Big chunks of the earth are in the rock swale water catchment system we had installed two years ago to divert water away from our one-level house. The water remains diverted. Our house is dry. The house is untouched, and our vehicles are mostly undamaged.

Big branches are down on our half-moon driveway and front yard. Every time I take a step, I lean over to pick up yet another big branch. It takes an hour to remove all of the branches from our short driveway. A giant tree blocks the road between our driveway and our next-door neighbors' driveway. There's a probably two-hundred-year-old oak tree fallen over in the road, and the branches are taller than we are. It's impossible to get out of our driveway.

We can hear our neighbor Kate already outside with her chainsaw, working diligently to cut up that tree. We call out over the fallen tree to her.

From Kate we learn that her husband, Erik, a firefighter and one of two rescue technicians for Gerton, left in his truck at 7:00 a.m. to make his way three miles down to the fire station, anticipating a busy day of helping people move fallen trees.

While Jeff and Kate continue to work on chopping up and moving that one fallen tree, which takes hours, I begin to assess damage in our eighty-five-acre HOA. Our HOA has eight houses: three full-time households and five part-time. Lots of trees are down on our shared road. No house sustained damage, but the road culverts are gone, and there are deep gashes in the road where water has run through it. There are three large mudslides covering the road. The two-mile road is impassable by anything but foot traffic. I check on our eighty-year-old neighbors, who seem in relatively good spirits. They have several trees down in their driveway and a giant chestnut tree leaning ominously over their house.

But while we are out checking on our neighborhood and chopping up trees, the power goes out. So does cell service. Kate can't get ahold of Erik. None of us can get ahold of anyone in the outside world. Both of our homes have whole house generators, so those kick on, offering us some semblance of normalcy when we go back inside.

We were due for a propane refill to fuel the generator before the hurricane. In fact, our delivery had been scheduled for three days after the hurricane, since we were down to 40 percent in our 500-gallon tank. We figure we will be fine and that power will be restored in a few days, as it always is. We don't yet know that *all* roads leading to our home have been destroyed, and that even if we needed it, a propane truck would be unable to make a delivery.

Erik finally arrives home around 5:00 p.m., by foot, wearing someone else's clothes. That's when we realized that things were much worse than we ever could have imagined.

## Day 2—9/28/24

We are trapped and isolated with no way out.

When Erik arrived home yesterday afternoon, he immediately told Kate to stop using her chainsaw. If she were to get hurt, he said, there would be no way to get her medical help.

"The roads below us are gone. Our small volunteer fire department has no contact with central command for our county. No one has cell phone service."

Erik hadn't even been able to make it the three miles down our mountain to the fire station, because trees kept falling in front of and behind him, as he was driving down in the early morning. Trees and power lines were falling at such an extreme rate that he didn't even have time to turn his truck off before evacuating the vehicle. He made his way to Jamie's house (another firefighter, rescue technician, and EMT who lives toward the bottom of our road) to get out of the dangerous environment this hurricane had created.

After the rain began tapering off around 11:00 a.m., Erik and Jamie spent the rest of the afternoon attempting to clear trees from our road and discovered that the road connecting ours to the main highway and fire station was completely gone, with a thirty-foot-deep chasm in its place, complete with waterfalls. It took them all day to clear trees off a half-mile stretch of our road. That's how many trees are down.

Jeff and I go over to Erik and Kate's house after Erik got home, because we are desperate for news and updates. We find both of them curled up on their living room sofa. Erik is teary eyed, like he has been crying, something I've never seen him do in the four years we've known each other. He is always stoic, a good match for his six-foot two-inch frame.

Erik tells us the devastation is overwhelming.

The day before and in preparation for what the hurricane might bring, Gerton and Bat Cave Fire Departments built a command center in Bat Cave, anticipating catastrophic flooding. It is common for fire departments and local authorities to consult flood maps before hurricanes make landfall to forecast potential damage.

A flood map is a topographical map that shows flood potential, highlighting river width and staging. Both flood and soil maps can be helpful in anticipating storm damage. We have loam soil here, making it easy to dig straight down into it to see how deep flooding has occurred. Soil maps show the soil horizon, the rate of flooding.

For our area, there is a one-hundred-year flood map (which still shows the impact of the Great Flood of 1916), a 500-year flood map, and a 1,000-year flood map, which shows the most extreme flooding over the past 1,000 years.

Expecting extensive damage, firefighters went door to door to people they knew personally in Gerton and Bat Cave, living along creeks and the river, having candid conversations, and encouraging them to evacuate. Many of them did leave, which saved their lives.

Erik says it will be months before our roads will be drivable and power will be restored. We believe him. We've heard Gerton referred to as "the bastard child of Henderson County." We know we will be last in our area to be helped. We are closer to Buncombe County than Henderson, and it's inconvenient for anyone to get here. We are often forgotten when it comes to road maintenance and other support.

# The Deep End of Hope in the Wake of Hurricane Helene

There is no communication with the outside world. Only a handful of Gerton firefighters are able to communicate with each other via emergency county radios. The rest of us have no way of contacting anyone, including family and loved ones.

These primarily volunteer first responders are bushwhacking through hollers and over mountains in the dark, trying to get to people to do wellness checks. It is heartbreaking. Tears fall down our cheeks as we sit in shock and disbelief.

Erik, Kate, Jeff, and I spend the rest of that first night sitting in the dark, talking through worst case scenarios, because there is no other way to respond to what we have learned. There is nonstop chatter through Erik's emergency radio, becoming the horrific background noise to this unfolding destruction.

No one in the outside world has any idea if we are okay. *I don't know if we're okay, either.*

We turn off our generators, because we no longer know when or if we'll get power restored. We hover around a single, battery-powered lamp, as if it could offer us warmth or comfort. The lamp reveals shadows of how we used to look, before this news. It is too much to take in all at once.

Today, when Jeff was out for hours clearing tree limbs and trying to get cell signal, I found myself paralyzed and anxious, unable to focus or do anything. I lay in bed but couldn't sleep. I haven't slept well since the heavy rain started four nights ago. Last night I got five hours straight, the most I've had. Not sleeping makes me cranky and makes me snap at Jeff.

Jeff has already leapt into action, assessing our resources, determining what we need to survive over the next couple of weeks, and creating a schedule for us of propane usage and daily activities. Overnight, he has become a stranger to me. Jeff already knows we are in this for the long haul. He has already submitted to this new way of operating. His heart has hardened to it, just like it did when he lived through Hurricane

Katrina in New Orleans. I am playing catch up, hoping he won't leave me behind.

Jeff and I become desperate for information, grilling Kate and Erik at night over dinner, comparing notes, trying to make sense of what has happened.

Kate and Erik were able to hike down to the fire station today in one hour, a trip that normally takes six minutes by car. They bushwhacked their way from our gate to the paved part of the road that connects ours to the highway. Apparently, there are big chunks missing from the paved road. In many places, it is undercut, with the ground beneath the pavement completely washed away.

Erik and Kate say there is no way our eighty-year-old neighbors, Paul and Susan, will be able to make it down the mountain. They are trapped here until the road is rebuilt or a helicopter comes to evacuate them. Paul and Susan do not have generator power and are already running out of food. They are cooking on a camp stove and using candles for light in their house.

Old Edward's tiny house survived, which is remarkable, because he lives in a holler, with a creek just a few feet away from his front door. But he also had a giant tree fall on his house two years ago, and never had it removed. The weight of that tree must have held his house in place, and the garbage bags piled up in his yard must have acted as sandbags, protecting the house from the high creek water.

Gloria and Russ's home made it as well, but the waterfall at the back of their property flooded the house. By 8:30 a.m. the morning of the hurricane, water, mud, and rocks as high as Gloria's knees surrounded the house. The road in front of their house had also become a raging river.

Their camper out back is encased in three feet of rocks, and the garage is filled with eight inches of mud. They can't use their kitchen door because rocks block it.

But all they could think about, when they saw the enormous quantity of water rushing down the waterfall and along the street in front of them, was their daughter Tarin and her three children.

Once the rain stopped midmorning, they walked a quarter mile down the road, in search of them. Tarin and her kids live along the same creek as Old Edward and on the same road as Gloria and Russ. They knew that Tarin's three kids and their pets were with their father, but Tarin told Gloria the night before that she was sheltering in place, despite Erik's pleas to evacuate because the creek was only a few feet from her house.

Tarin's vehicle was there, but she was nowhere to be found. The house had a giant tree through it. The tree, combined with rushing creek water, ripped away half of the house, including the entire basement. Gloria and Russ feared the worst, that she had been washed away by the rushing water.

Later that day Gloria learned that Tarin's friend David had driven to her house in the storm the night before, to get her out of there. Gloria still tears up recounting those hours when she didn't know if her daughter was alive.

The night following the hurricane, Tarin got into a car accident. With no streetlights, she was driving in the pitch black, and came upon a dark-colored car, abandoned in the middle of the mud-covered highway. She tried to stop, but her vehicle slid into the back of the nearly invisible car. We don't know yet if she's okay.

I hate hearing this news, but it is comforting to know that so far, everyone we know is at least still alive.

The fire station did not sustain damage. The post office and community center both flooded but may be fixable. The Baptist church looks like nothing even happened to it. People walking by stop and stare at the church, wondering how it miraculously escaped damage.

## Emma Churchman, MDiv

There is a giant mudslide covering the highway, between the fire station and Bearwallow Provision Company (BearProCo). Kate watches our friend Scott scaling the mudslide using clothing racks taken from BearProCo to navigate the terrain. They are placed over the mud to create traction and to keep people from falling into the mud.

He is dressed in a white, long sleeved linen shirt, flannel pajama pants, and hiking boots. Scott is always fashionably dressed. It doesn't surprise me in the slightest that he's created his own disaster apparel.

It's 10:00 a.m., and he's drinking a can of wine that he got out of BearProCo, precariously risking his life to get inside the store before the roof collapsed. Like many of us, he has a prepaid account. I guess he wants to use it while he still can.

We spend weeks teasing Scott mercilessly about the can of wine. But the truth is, he was just trying to cope in this new reality, like we all are. Sometimes that looks like drinking wine at 10:00 a.m. while scaling a mudslide covering the highway wearing jammies.

BearProCo is a critical fixture in our tiny community. For over four years, it has been a gathering place in the Gerton community, bringing together residents as well as tourists. The community depended on this shop as a meeting place, a musical venue, and a location to hang out and enjoy one another.

It is devastating to know it was destroyed.

Erik works with Scott and a few others to build a bridge out of a giant, heavy dining room table, donated by another resident. The table had been sitting in their basement for years. The temporary bridge replaces a road that was washed away by the creek-turned-river that runs behind our community center. There are people on the other side who need medication, and first responders can't get to them without this bridge.

Toward the end of the day, Erik and his crew are also able to begin clearing the road up to Little Pisgah, the other mountain in our fire district. They encounter a big mudslide about a half mile up and without heavy equipment have to stop there for the day.

Every rescue is urgent. Every wellness check matters. But only a handful of people are working all day long to get to as many people as possible. All roads are destroyed. Mudslides block every turn. Everything is taking too much time.

In my mind I'm trying to picture what we will see when we accompany Erik and Kate down the mountain. I am preparing myself for the worst. If I can imagine it, then maybe it won't be as hard to see the devastation in person.

## Day 3—9/29/24

This morning, I have resolved to wake up and do things differently. Once we turn on the generator for its morning two-hour run, I make myself three hot beverages and plan out dinner with Jeff. I use the bathroom multiple times (and flush the toilet!), because I can during this small window of time.

Then I sit down at the dining room table with all the lights on, and work on a puzzle with Jeff, while listening to music. I had no idea what a huge difference listening to music would be. It was a moment of normalcy in the midst of chaos.

My anxiety has been extremely high since Wednesday night. It is now Monday morning. Having two hours of normal this morning with the generator on, helps.

Kate and other locals continue to try and get up the road to the top of Little Pisgah. They know of a ninety-four-year-old man and several other older people who live at the top of this three-and-a-half-mile road, and want to deliver water and food to them. Kate, Collin, and DJ ride to the road in the bucket of a John Deere tractor driven by firefighter Jacob, carrying water and food with them. They make the best of the situation, having fun during the moments they can.

Jacob lives on his family compound with his wife, Erin, in a green house, with flowers outside, lovingly planted by Erin. His father and twin brothers live in the other house on the property. A giant mudslide hacked out a section of the mountain behind their homes and flooded all around them, reaching as high as the bottom porch steps.

The bridge from their compound to the main road washed out completely. Jacob's grandfather built the bridge many years ago by securing two tractor trailer beds together (minus tires) and then adhering them to a giant rock lodged underneath the road's surface. The creek under the bridge grew from a few feet wide to over thirty feet in a matter of hours.

During the hurricane, Jacob worked at the fire station up the highway in Fairview. He wasn't able to get home to Gerton until this morning and only then by ATV. He didn't know if his wife, father, and brothers were alive, or if any damage had happened to their property. He feared the worst.

On the Little Pisgah Road, Jacob and another firefighter each operate tractors to clear what turns out to be multiple mudslides. A concerned family member of someone who lives in Middle Fork (on the other side of the mountain) joins the crew to help cut and clear trees. There are also people trying to clear an old logging road from the other side of the mountain, hoping to meet halfway.

By tomorrow, we hope, the entire logging road will be cleared all of the way to Middle Fork. The first delivery of supplies from the outside, including water, MREs (meals ready to eat), and snacks will be brought to the one hundred residents there via UTV, as all of their roads were destroyed.

Jeff's satellite GPS gadget that we use for hiking gives us the weather report. Having that information is comforting. We have some idea of what to expect. We are not completely in the dark and out of control. We were so worried that more rain was coming, but sunny skies are predicted for the foreseeable future.

Jeff and I spend a few hours sitting in Erik and Kate's field on this gorgeous, blue-sky day. Jeff sometimes has cell service here. We see a large, black military helicopter fly above us. I burst into tears, knowing that help must be on the way. It is the first indication that the outside world understands the extent of our devastation.

We cannot get any outside news. We don't know if the president has determined this to be a federal disaster. We don't know if FEMA (Federal Emergency Management Agency) is involved. We don't know if more military are on their way. Gerton is *so* low on the priority list of places to fix that it could be months before our power is restored. MONTHS. We have no idea how we will get our private road fixed. There is no way our regular road contractor can handle rebuilding, plus there is no way for him to even get to the road.

Our fire department still has no contact with central command for our county or with anyone else in the area. We are completely isolated. Erik's mother somehow made contact with the Henderson County Sheriff yesterday, trying to tell them to come rescue us. We don't need to be rescued. I think she's just anxious that she hasn't been able to speak with Erik. She is able to get text messages to him through Jeff's phone.

Jeff's phone has become our command central as he relays messages for all four of us and starts responding to questions on his "We are Gerton, NC" Facebook group. Family members, desperate for information about their loved ones, started reaching out via this group in increasing numbers. Little did we know that Jeff's one phone would become the way for all of Gerton's residents and their families to communicate with one another.

There are no operational roads from the county sheriff's office to Gerton. We did learn yesterday that the road from Gerton to Fairview where our grocery and post office are is clear, which is how supplies were delivered, but we have no way to access that road or even get off our mountain. Our cars sit like museum pieces next to our house.

Last night Jeff got some strong cell service inside our house. We thought maybe phone calls would be possible, as so far, all our communication has been via texting on his phone or via Facebook. I tried calling my dentist and my hair salon to cancel my appointments for this coming week. That's when we learned that all phone lines are down in Asheville. We got error messages for both businesses. I guess they are shut down, too.

We made contact with Jeff's mother and brother in Fairview through texts from our mutual friend Chase, who was able to check on them, but we haven't spoken with them directly. All we know is some trees fell on Linda's house and in her yard, but there is no apparent damage to the house itself, and their water pressure is low.

We are also able to make contact with several neighbors out of the area who have their second homes in our neighborhood. All five couples tell us to raid their homes and take everything we need: food, liquor, batteries, flashlights and candles, chainsaws, gas, propane, really anything we could find that might be of use to us during this time. My heart grows bigger simply being offered what they wouldn't need.

We go house by house cleaning out fridges in some instances and discarding food before it goes bad or holding onto it to consume in the coming weeks. Bobby and Meredith's pork loins are a big hit and easy for us to cook on our outside grill, which is helpful because we are conserving propane use. We raid their candy stash too and begin consuming it as if it is crack cocaine. The sugar gives us energy in the evenings when we are too tired to keep our eyes open, and the four of us are huddled in the dark, debriefing the day and making plans.

Don and Laura's chainsaw becomes invaluable, as ours refuses to start. There are so many trees down on our shared roads, and we want to start clearing as many of them as possible, once we know we can get medical help if needed. Just knowing that we have supplies and resources available to us here without having to make a six-mile trek down and up our mountain, eases our minds considerably.

We have gotten disconcertingly good at living in this new way, over too short an amount of time. We've figured out how to operate with almost no cell service, how to gather supplies and information, and how to run our household with limited generator power.

Jeff and I decided this morning to spend two full weeks here before hiking out with what we can carry on our backs, plus the dogs and what they need.

As of now, we have no idea where we will go. We don't know what exists anymore. Roads are gone. According to the Duke Energy outage map, this entire part of the state has no power.

No grocery stores are open. Nothing is open. No gasoline is available. There were rumors yesterday that cases of water will be made available in the Food Lion parking lot in Fairview. But we don't need water, our well is still operational when our generator is on. Also, we can't get to Fairview anyway.

We cannot get information from the outside world. We don't really know anything that is happening more than a few miles away from us. Even information from the next town over is sparse. The not knowing makes this so much harder. *How many people were affected by the hurricane? When is help going to arrive?*

Every day at the Gerton Fire Department there is a 9:00 a.m. planning meeting and a 1:00 p.m. community meeting, to check in, hear the news, and assign tasks. Community is being built, but Erik and Kate also said it's starting to be like the Wild West down there. People are beginning to feel desperate for resources, and we are only three full days into this. Erik and Kate are both bringing their guns down with them today. Jeff was going to go with them, but we both got so worried when we woke up this morning about getting injured while bush-whacking, and then exhausted hiking down and up for three miles each way, that we decided he wouldn't go with them.

It was the right decision. Our priority needs to be ensuring that we are physically safe and able to care for each other, the dogs, and our home, and get connected with the outside world for more information about resources coming to help us. Jeff is spending most of the day in communications with the outside world via his Facebook group. It's strangely quiet here on the mountain at times, but at other times, helicopters fly over just a few feet above our house. We want to monitor what is happening.

We also don't want to leave our home and property unless absolutely necessary, because we're already hearing horror stories of looting or of random people showing up at neighbors' houses late at night carrying AK-47s. Welcome to the gun show. We're living it right now.

Each day I work on my lists:

1. **Generator Checklist** - things to do when we have power.

2. **Evacuation Packing List and House Checklist** - how to shut down the house before we leave.

3. **Propane Measurements** - tracking our usage so we know how much is left. The percentage remaining drops by two to three percentage points a day.

4. **The Outside World** - who to contact and what information to gather so we know what resources are coming to us.

5. **Future Disaster Planning** - what we want to have in place should a disaster like this happen again. At the top of the list are a drone and walkie-talkies. Not knowing what is going on around us is terrifying.

These lists help me feel like I can make some sense of what is happening. For a few minutes a day, I can feel in control of something.

Prior to this, I had been praying for ways to stop watching TV so much, to not be on my phone or the internet so much, to not distract myself so much. Well, that time has come to me by way of an apocalypse.

I keep reminding myself that everything happening is happening *for* me. This lack of connectivity is a gift.

Then there is the gift of becoming even closer with Erik and Kate. The gift of becoming more of a team with Jeff and deepening our friendship and capacity to function well together. The gift of weeks away from client delivery, so that I can return to myself. The gift of evolving as a human. The gift of not having to be "productive" in the ways I am used to, for days and weeks. The gift of not opening my computer.

Challenge can make us bitter or better. This is the foundational orientation of a traumatic response. I choose to allow the trauma to empower me, not shrink me.

My intuition is telling me that this catastrophic hurricane is showing me there is another way forward for my life. It's about living life, not living for work. Life comes first. Family comes first. Community comes first. Writing comes first.

I am writing my way through this apocalypse.

# Day 4 of the Apocalypse—9/30/24

This is the message I put out on Jeff's Facebook page today, via his phone, as my phone still doesn't work, and I can't access my Facebook account:

"Hurricane Helene was catastrophic for residents of Western North Carolina. We are living in an apocalypse.

"We are safe. Our home did not sustain damage. We have dozens of trees down on our property and road as well as multiple landslides.

"We live on top of a mountain and are without power or internet. We are rationing propane usage for our generator. At this time, we still have food and can access our well water when we run the generator.

"I have no phone, email, or Facebook access. I hiked five miles down the mountain today to be able to post this on my husband's page via an emergency Wi-Fi signal.

"The roads below us are either destroyed or washed out and are unusable by foot or vehicle.

"The only way out for us is to bushwhack three miles down the mountain with our dogs to the fire station for rescue.

"We plan on evacuating when our propane runs out. Meanwhile our neighbors who were not here during the hurricane have allowed us to raid their homes for provisions. They have been an incredible lifeline for us.

"Our next-door neighbor is a firefighter and rescue technician. Every day he and his wife Kate go out to rescue people who are trapped in our fire district. Jeff and I are focusing on helping our local community hear news from the outside world and communicate with loved ones, as Jeff's phone is the only one on the mountain with any service, and it is spotty at best.

"Hickory Nut Gorge, where we live, was hit incredibly hard. So many houses and businesses were washed away by the flooding, and many people are trapped in their homes. As of today, we have not heard of any fatalities in our community.

"Our small community of Gerton, NC has 300 residents, and is about thirty minutes south of Asheville, NC. We are extremely isolated. Yesterday four people from Homeland Security were finally able to get to our fire station to begin to assess damage.

"Because of our small size and location, we expect to be one of the last places to have power restored and roads fixed. It may be months before we get help.

"I just burst into tears when I saw a Black Hawk helicopter fly directly over our house while I wrote this message. I am grateful that help is on the way."

---

Lots of people commented that they have been checking Facebook every day, wondering if I was still alive. People who I didn't even think would pay attention are filling my feed and my DMs. They are all praying. They are all sending Love. They are asking how to help.

*The outside world knows what is happening! They recognize how catastrophic the hurricane was!*

I am disconcertingly joyous.

Jeff and I talk about how to best be of service to our community during this time. He seems to be the only one on our mountain with any cell service, albeit spotty. Jeff also is the administrator of the "We are Gerton, NC" Facebook group, which he established three years ago. For those three years it has had forty-five members. Jeff decided that he would start disseminating information about Gerton via this Facebook group, so that people would know what is happening here. Overnight, people started joining this group in record numbers, desperate to know about their loved ones, their homes and property, and the state of the devastation.

Before the hurricane Jeff, Erik, Kate, and I used to joke about what we would do if an apocalypse ever happened. This came out of observing a subsect of our community that calls themselves the Gerton Guard, a conservative group of primarily men. They deeply believe that if the world ended, our tiny town of Gerton would be hit the hardest. They are all Preppers, with an abundance of MREs, guns, generators, and off-grid living tools at their disposal.

We always thought that was far-fetched. Surely bigger towns like Washington, DC, New York, or San Francisco would be hit the hardest in an apocalypse?

Turns out the Gerton Guard was right.

In our joking, we imagined what each of our roles would be. For Erik and Kate, it was fairly obvious. Erik is a firefighter and rescue first responder. Kate has mad chainsaw skills and is a botanist. For Jeff and me, the roles were more subtle. Jeff is infinitely resourceful, the smartest person I know, and is a fantastic communicator. Jeff's impetus is to fix everything. Plus, he had the Katrina experience. Mine is to ask everyone how they are feeling and bear witness to their pain. Both things matter right now.

Jeff has become chief communicator to the outside world and has begun coordinating supplies being brought in via his Facebook group, as our fire department still has no cell or internet service. I have become the self-appointed, volunteer trauma chaplain, something I haven't done in nearly ten years.

# Day 5 of the Apocalypse

We hiked down to the fire station yesterday for the first time. Erik and Kate guided us through the narrow path in neighbors 'yards and fields that allows us to bypass the destroyed roads. It was a beautiful, horrendous walk.

The walk is peaceful and absolutely quiet. Everything is so quiet here, especially first thing in the morning, before the helicopters start flying overhead. We don't even hear birds chirping.

Fall has come to our mountain, usually my favorite time of year. The road going up our mountain should already be busy. Tourists arrive here in droves each year to see the fall colors. But instead, there is no sound and no movement.

Seeing the devastation revealed a foot at a time makes it somehow easier to take in than if we were driving through it. But the devastation is everywhere. It is impossible to escape.

We run into people on the way to the fire station. It feels good to see people we know. There is an instant knowing and understanding between us. We are in this together. We stop by people's houses to check on them or see them wandering the street like we are. We exchange information, well wishes, and hugs.

Jeff is able to get critical information to people that he's collected from his Facebook group. We stop by Billy's house to tell him that his daughter is enroute to see him. She'll be here tomorrow. Billy tears up with this news.

Today I spoke at our daily community meeting down at the fire station to a crowd of about seventy people.

"My name is Emma Churchman and I'm a trauma chaplain.

"I want to take a few minutes to speak with you all about what we have experienced as a community.

"Regardless of what you have been through over the past five days, you have experienced a life-changing, will-never-return-to-normal-again traumatic event.

"Maybe your home or your property was damaged. Maybe a neighbor or a loved one you know is suffering. Maybe the rescue and the recovery work that you've been doing has shown you things you have never had to deal with before.

"Maybe you didn't personally experience any damage. It doesn't matter. Each of us has had a traumatic experience.

"We are here because a hurricane tore through our Gorge and had its way with us.

"This is a once-in-a-lifetime devastation that will change each of us and the community of Gerton and will impact us for the rest of our lives.

"We are different people today than we were a week ago.

"It's normal to feel out of place as a result. It's normal to *not* know how to exist.

"What you are doing here today is so important. You are choosing to come together as a community. You are finding ways to work together and to be of help.

"You are partaking in the amazing resources that are being showered on us right now by people outside of Gerton. Every time you accept help, you are blessing the person who is giving to you. You are helping us to come together as a larger community.

"As a trauma chaplain my role is to listen to you and support you, regardless of what religion you are, or whether or not you are religious. I am specifically experienced in helping people through situations just like what we're going through right now.

"But here's the thing about being in the middle of a catastrophic event: It's hard to understand in the moment that you are experiencing a stress response.

"I want to give you some markers to look for, so you know if you're having a trauma response, which of course is normal. You may feel one, two, or all of these. Just know this is normal for what you have experienced.

- You can only remember one thing at a time. You start walking to do something but then someone starts talking to you, and you completely forget what you were going to do.

- You feel anxious when you did not have a lot of anxiety before.

- You seem to be doing okay, but then all of a sudden, you're overcome with anger or with sadness. You may start yelling or crying. Then it passes, and you can't figure out what made you angry or sad.

- You get obsessive about creating a routine for yourself. For example, you have to wake up at a certain time or turn on your generator at the same time every day, or keep your house organized a certain way.

- You get really upset at other people and how they are handling the hurricane catastrophe. You think they should be responding differently.

- You keep repeating the same stories about what you have experienced because you are trying to make sense of them.
- You're drinking a lot more than normal.
- You're not sleeping, or you're only sleeping for a few hours each night.
- You're having apocalyptic dreams of being trapped or running out of food.

"If you're going through any of the things I've described, you aren't crazy, and there is nothing wrong with you. You are having a very normal response to a very abnormal event.

"Your body, mind, and heart are trying to process what has happened. You're trying to find ways to cope and get through this.

"If you find yourself responding in ways that you don't normally, or if you feel out of control or out of sorts, please come talk with me.

"I am here to help by talking with you about what you're going through and help you figure out how to deal with this new reality that we are in.

"If you like, I am here to pray with you and bless you.

"We also don't have to talk. You can just touch me on the shoulder or squeeze my hand so that I know you are going through some of the things I just spoke about, and I can hold you in my prayers.

"I am here to be with you in this and will help any way I can. I will be here every day if I can at 1:00 p.m. and for a few hours afterward if you want to connect with me."

I watch people look at me after the meeting, but very few approach me directly. It takes me a while to realize what's happening. Many of these people either don't know me at all or don't have the bandwidth to introduce themselves.

Even worse, many of them don't yet realize that they are traumatized.

# Day 6 of the Apocalypse

There is a campground a few miles down from us in Bat Cave, next to the highway and along a creek. We know there were a number of people there, but no one has been able to make contact with them.

The campground is owned by the assistant fire chief, a man named Aaron, but he hadn't been responding by radio to wellness checks. It became a priority to get to the campground by Day 3 and check for medical emergencies.

It takes Erik and Jamie two hours to hike there because the highway is gone. In its stead, a boulder-filled, muddy mess remains. Jamie and Erik stop to check on people and houses enroute. Up until Day 3, no one had traveled more than one mile south of the Gerton Fire Station. Many people are still unaccounted for.

They navigate the wide swath of rubble, comprising what used to be the road and the Hickory Creek, which ran alongside it. Both the road and creek were nestled in the crevice of our Gorge. The rubble has multiple mudslides, hundreds of fallen trees and power lines, and farther down, obliterated homes and cars strewn along it. It is almost impassable, even by foot. Multiple times, Erik and Jamie have to hike around the rubble, because of deep cavernous holes where the road used to be.

All the water from streams and creeks above the campground converge right by it. The result is massive flooding. The water erased some of the cabins and destroyed others. A huge mudslide from the mountain behind the campground also wiped-out sections. A few days after the hurricane, the creek-turned-river is now only about thirty feet wide, with the riverbed clearly marking a one-hundred-foot expanse. Jamie and Erik hike through the deep water.

The scene they encountered on the other side of the river is unimaginable. People at the campsite are actively experiencing post-traumatic stress. They are distant, confused, and walking around like zombies. Both firefighters find themselves very wary at the campground, because everyone is acting so strangely. Stunned. Glazed over. Not able to engage or comprehend well. We would come to know this look well in subsequent days.

They discover that there are several tourists who had been staying at the campground. The tourists knew the hurricane was headed our way, but they stayed anyway. They are now desperate to leave because they have no power or water. There is raw sewage covering the ground, because all the black water tanks have filled. It is cataclysmic.

Erik and Jamie can't get good information from these people who are in the freeze response, a post-trauma state we used to refer to as shock. They are trying to find Aaron. No one seems to know *who* or *where* he is. One of the people tells Jamie and Erik that a woman in a house on the other side of the road is having a medical emergency. No one knew whether Aaron had attended to the woman. No one knew anything.

They finally find Aaron and he too seems to be in shock. All he's able to tell Erik and Jamie is that he could hear everything going on as he listened on his emergency county radio: all of the transmissions between Erik, Jamie, and the other firefighters, but no one could hear him. He says he is doubting his sanity.

And there is no way out of the campground. It is blocked on one side by a mountain mudslide, on the other side by the creek-turned-river that is still raging.

Erik and Jamie are called away to another emergency, so they gather supplies and leave instructions with six people at the campground to create a temporary footbridge across the creek to a field where they will be evacuated.

The other emergency turns out to have already been handled the day prior by Rob and Jenn, married firefighters and EMTs from Bat Cave. That's how challenging communications were the first few days. No one knew anything. Information was always delayed, broken, or nonexistent.

They reported that in the late afternoon on Day 1, Rob and Jenn took a call to rescue families living in Trillium Court, which is technically located in Gerton but closer to Bat Cave. Three houses had collapsed into each other, following a mudslide down the mountain. Multiple people sustained injuries, some of which were life-threatening. They also learned at least one child was trapped.

Rob, Jenn, and their eighteen-year-old son, Danann, a junior firefighter, had already spent all day running around in their immediate community, Middle Fork, conducting wellness checks. So far, everyone was safe. They have a daughter down in Lake Lure they hadn't heard from. They didn't know if she was alive, and yet they set their fears aside as they prepared to help multiple families.

Rob is retired Army Special Forces and an expert at land navigation. Jenn has recently completed many technical rescue courses, including one on helicopter rescues. Rob has a FirstNet phone, which means his cell phone is able to utilize all cell phone towers in the area. They also have county emergency radios, a medical pack, and a CalTopo mapping platform. The digital platform enables them to plot a course over Burntshirt Mountain, from their house to Trillium Court. They made the hard decision to leave their other daughter, a fifteen-year-old, at home with a radio, so they could keep in touch. Rob and Jenn had no idea how long it would be before they were able to return home.

The two-and-a-half-mile hike took them two-and-a-half hours, even though they were rushing, because they had to bushwhack through tall rhododendron and mountain laurel thickets. They reached the houses about thirty minutes after dark, exhausted.

As they neared, they saw a giant mudslide had forced the homes off of their foundations. A river of water was flowing all around the houses. The highway below them was destroyed in both directions. Creeks had been diverted across the road. They came to the harrowing conclusion that there was no way to hike the survivors out.

When they arrived, the survivors had gathered inside a white house, about 150 yards from the three collapsed houses. Tara and Jim's house, a second home for them, was unscathed. Tara and Jim had a couple staying with them, who had evacuated to the mountains from Florida to try and get away from Helene. The four of them were also physically unscathed.

One young couple was able to escape their home, the first to be hit by the mudslide, with only the clothes on their backs, not even shoes. The woman was hysterical and inconsolable.

The second house was turned on its side, ninety degrees, as the first house hit it. A mother and three children were inside. The three-year-old and twelve-year-old got out, but the mother and nine-year-old were trapped.

The man inside of the third collapsed house sustained significant injuries to his ribs, and possibly lungs, but was able to get out.

Before Rob and Jenn arrived, Rich, a neighbor from Bat Cave, heard the survivors crying for help. Rich, a Brit who now lives in the US, and his wife own two rental properties in Bat Cave. The first, an A-frame house along the highway, sits along the Rocky Broad River in downtown Bat Cave. His wife and children were in Florida, and he was sleeping in the house during the hurricane, as he was preparing it to be an Airbnb rental. The first guests were scheduled to arrive in a few days.

Rich awoke at 3:00 a.m. to see the river rising quickly. Fearing the worst, he evacuated with a backpack full of clothes, food, and his laptop. He was able to drive to his second rental property, a half mile north on the highway, and a few doors up from the fire station. The house was farther from the river, but on a creek. He slept for a few hours and woke to discover the creek levels had risen, and a microwind event (which he described as a tornado) had ripped the deck off of the house into six pieces.

Rich checked in at the fire station and saw his neighbor Mike, who had evacuated from his home on the river. Mike was visibly shaken, having felt the impact of the water against his house. Together, Mike and Rich watched as Mike's home fell into the river and floated away. Rich then rushed to check on his A-frame house along the same river. It was gone. His neighbors were there and said they had just watched it float away as well. Rich was stunned by the devastation but more concerned about the well-being of his neighbors and getting home to his wife and kids in Florida.

After checking in with his neighbors and letting people at the fire station know they were okay, Rich decided to attempt to evacuate. He was wearing hiking boots, shorts, a light, fleece top, and a fluorescent green waterproof jacket given to him by a neighbor.

He began hiking up the highway toward Gerton, hoping to make it to the Gerton Fire Station, four miles away. Each mile took about an hour, as there were landslides every couple of hundred feet. The deep mud, combined with downed trees and power lines, made the trip challenging. Rich's years of snowboarding and navigating snow equipped him to be able to walk through the mud fairly effectively.

He made it to just shy of Trillium Court, about 2.2 miles. He climbed over a giant mudslide and saw a wild boar trapped in the mud. The boar wrestled his way free, and then stood and blocked Rich's path, looking angry. Eventually the boar moved on. Rich saw above him a white house with a car behind it, so he began shouting, to see if anyone needed help. People shouted back.

It took him twenty minutes to get through the landslide, which had mud up to twenty feet deep. Even with his six-foot, six-inch frame, Rich was struggling. Near the white house, he saw chickens and a couple of dogs wandering around.

Rich went to assist a neighbor trying to get the mother out of the second collapsed house. Both of her legs were injured. They extricated her by pulling her out on a mattress.

Her nine-year-old daughter was pinned between a floor and a wall, with one leg sticking out a window full of broken glass. She had been in that position for seven hours and was only able to move one arm. Rich spent three hours digging her out, stopping once to give her the food and water he had, because she hadn't had any since the night before.

He and one of the survivors worked to cut away the aluminum window frame and remove the glass to prevent further injury to the girl. By the end, Rich's body was covered in cuts, and he was bleeding everywhere. He was terrified the girl would die before he could get her out.

The survivor brought a car jack from his home, and Rich wedged it between the wall and the ground, lifting the wall about ten inches. Only then was he able to finally extricate the girl.

Rich has five children of his own and was doing whatever it took to help this girl. In these types of situations, this is just what happens: People do whatever it takes to jump in and help. Regardless of background, of history with the people needing help, of personal levels of exhaustion, or mental state or fear, people help. This is what allowed all of us to make it through the first week before additional help and resources showed up. All day long, we did whatever we could to make a difference, save people, and save ourselves.

It turns out that Rich has no experience with emergencies or natural disasters. In fact, he is a vice president at a major office supply company.

## The Deep End of Hope in the Wake of Hurricane Helene

By the time Rob, Jenn, and Danann arrive, Tara is already attending to her neighbors, bandaging and cleaning them up as best she can, giving them dry clothes, and feeding them out of her dwindling food and potable water supply.

Jenn assesses each person, taking vitals, and splinting injuries. She notes that the lungs sounded clear on the man with the broken ribs, who also had a concussion and laceration on his head. The nine-year-old had a probable leg and/or ankle fracture. The three-year-old had lacerations on his back and arms. The young couple both had lacerations on their feet. All survivors witnessed and were traumatized by the force and sound of the mudslide that took their homes. The children were especially fearful of a repeat slide that night.

There were trapped animals, including a dog that was inside a room of one of the collapsed houses, as well as cats, chickens, and the "wild boar," who turned out to be a pet of one of the families. Rich had tried to free the dog, but it was too dangerous. The dog cried on and off throughout the night, which upset everyone, especially the three-year-old child.

Rob made contact with the county, determining it would be easier to evacuate everyone by Black Hawk helicopter in the morning, with better visibility. Rich calmed down the kids by telling them stories. Tara offered mothering to everyone. Their services were compassionate and incredibly helpful.

Rob, Jenn, and Danann stayed in Tara and Jim's RV behind their house and were able to sleep for a few hours. The survivors all slept on the main floor of Tara's house.

In the morning, the dog was evacuated from the collapsed house, and the Black Hawk arrived, hovering above the houses. Rob was able to speak directly with the pilot, advising him where to land the basket to ensure safety for the survivors and helicopter. Everyone, including Rich, was evacuated by basket, two by two, except Tara and Jim, who wanted to stay to attend to their home before hiking out for rescue.

Rob, Jenn, and Danann made the four-and-a-half-hour hike home, around the mountain this time. Rob was able to text family members of all the survivors to let them know they were safely evacuated. Finally home and able to hug their daughter, they were exhausted, but knew there was much more to be done to help many other people still unaccounted for.

The second day of the campground rescue, Erik returned only to discover the footbridge had *not* been built. Nothing was done. The people were in too much shock to follow yesterday's basic instructions. This is normal in a traumatic situation. The brain stops working. It's impossible to figure out how to get from A to B, or add, or process complex steps.

Erik built the bridge out of picnic tables. He and a few others cleared the field enough to create a landing zone, so people could be evacuated by helicopter.

Criteria for evacuation changed in the wake of Helene. Before, there was rigorous criteria involving primarily medical emergencies. But for this particular evacuation, it included people who needed medical help, along with people who might not be able to care for themselves (like the elderly), along with nonresidents (i.e., people who had just been camping). Without power, food, shelter, water, or access to any resources, the criteria had to expand.

Thirty-two people were evacuated from the campground in multiple trips five days after the hurricane. It took that long to rescue them as space had to be cleared for a Black Hawk helicopter to hover above and then evacuate people by basket.

The campground was Aaron's family's primary source of income. Aaron's insurance refuses to pay for repairs because he didn't have flood insurance. *Of course he didn't have flood insurance because we live in the mountains, three hundred miles from the coast!* This is the first we hear of the hundreds of stories of people turned down by their insurance companies because they didn't have flood insurance.

Aaron, a big guy who chuckles loudly, keeps nervously laughing as he tells me that he doesn't know what to do next with the campground. Tourism is gone from the area with the catastrophic damage. He doesn't have the money to fix everything himself. He, like everyone, has more questions than answers right now.

# Day 7 of the Apocalypse
## Gerton, NC, Pop. 300

This Apocalypse has blessed me with a wealth of new-to-me experiences. As I learn to navigate the post-hurricane reality we are living in our small, rural community in Western North Carolina, every day presents new ways of being present.

I'm not alone in the new experiences. Jeff has quickly become a morning person for the first time in his life, because now we both get up at 7:00 a.m. to turn on the generator for two hours. We need to carefully time powering our refrigerator and freezer, so food doesn't spoil. I am learning to share my sacred, early morning hours with him. It is not going well. We are both cranky and sleep deprived.

Each morning, I refer to the generator checklist to remind myself of what to do, because every morning, right on cue, I forget.

- Eat. Shit. Shower. Too vulgar? So is the devastation we are living in.
- Charge cell phones and battery-operated lights.
- Check propane level.
- Send messages out via Jeff's cell phone.

It's not like it's a long list. My brain simply cannot retain information like that right now. That's the way with a trauma response.

In the mornings, we also refill containers to have access to drinking water during the day. In our kitchen sink is a large metal bowl that we refill with hot water and soap, for dirty dishes. A similar, smaller bowl gets refilled next to the bathroom sink for handwashing.

We save laundry and running the dishwasher for the evening, when we turn on the generator for a generous three hours, which allows us enough time to wash and dry one load of laundry and run the dishwasher on a full cycle.

We now use the clock on our stove to track how many hours we've had the generator running each morning and evening. As everyone knows, when the power goes out, the clock blinks at 12:00. I never found this useful and was always irritated by having to reset it. Turns out, it very handily counts up the minutes and hours that our generator has been on, starting with 12:00. In the morning, we run it to 2:00, in the evenings until 3:00.

Our bathtub remains filled with water in the event our propane runs out and we lose access to our well water by not being able to power our pump.

Jeff just uses a flashlight to find clothes in our master closet while the generator is running, because operating in the dark has become more familiar to him than having electricity.

Our TV time is now sitting in camp chairs in our neighbors' field watching different types of helicopters fly over us. I can now identify the helicopter type by look and sound because there are so many flying low to the ground above us twenty-four hours a day. They are the background music to our horror story.

Our daily, three-mile hike down our mountain to the fire station requires that we walk under widow-maker fallen trees, over downed power lines, and around mudslides. It is the highlight of our day just being in the quiet beauty of the fall, which still shines through the devastation. We are simply present to what is right in front of us and the journey becomes devotion time for the four of us.

Jeff is coordinating with the children of our eighty-year-old neighbors Paul and Susan to get them evacuated by helicopter. We now know how to set up a regulation helicopter landing area in a field.

We continue to raid our neighbors' homes. We take flashlights with us, because even during the day, it is dark inside some of the houses. We carry out what we can in our hiking packs. We are good raiders.

Every day we focus on getting things done so that this catastrophe doesn't last one minute longer than it needs to.

Our neighbor Walter and his son Peter drove up from Charleston to bring us food, gas, and cash. They spend two nights up here, inviting us over to their gas-powered-generator home and cooking for us. We had never been inside their home before. It feels good to be in community with them, to have a few hours of eating dinner at a neighbor's house, like normal people. Despite being in his seventies, Walter helps us clear trees off our private road. Peter donates his services to our community as an ER doctor for residents in need. He and I have the chance to work together to attend to one patient.

Down at the fire station, hundreds of volunteers are milling around. They drive in daily now, wanting to help, from as far away as Oklahoma. Many of them drop off supplies; some bring in chainsaws and willing hands to help move trees off roads and houses. Others donate ATVs or their excavators and other heavy equipment, to help rebuild roads.

Mennonite Disaster Service shows up to remove trees off houses. I get a kick out of introducing myself to them as a Quaker minister. Finally, I am an Anabaptist among Anabaptists, not a common occurrence in this part of the country.

I watch at least fifty truckloads of gravel drive by the fire station today to begin restoration on the road between Gerton and Bat Cave.

I chat with our neighbor DJ a few times as he's coming back from missions. DJ is twenty-four years old, slight of build, with long brown hair, usually tied back in a ponytail, and glasses. He is a butcher at Hickory Nut Gap Farm in Fairview, run by the Ager family.

DJ has been in the thick of rescue and recovery work since Day 1, often accompanying Erik or Kate on missions. He's also run a few missions himself, including taking a doctor on wellness checks in Bat Cave, and checking on people and delivering supplies in Middle Fork via an ATV path. Middle Fork is a part of our Fire District that has absolutely no road access where about one hundred people live.

DJ's home already has mold from the hurricane. During the storm, the propane tank that runs their generator got dislodged. It was pushed by a mudslide into a large pond next to their house, so DJ and his parents have no power. DJ's car was also buried in the mudslide. But DJ's spirit is incredible. He immediately says "Yes" anytime someone asks for help.

Today enroute to the fire station, I passed by a whole posse of the Ager family with chainsaws on the ATV path that has now been cut through our neighbors' property. We use this path to bypass the section of road that is now a thirty-foot-deep chasm.

The Agers ask me where to go to cut fallen trees. I direct them to a cluster of houses that has massive tree damage. I am impressed that even in the midst of dealing with their own devastation at the farm, their impetus is to serve.

During today's community meeting, we have a long conversation about what to do with all of the residential and storm trash piling up, because there is no trash service. There is talk of getting a communal dumpster, to bridge the gap until trash service can resume. It will take a miracle for that to resume this year.

I've been hitching a lot of rides between a section of paved road below us and the fire station, as well as between the fire station and the "checkpoint." The checkpoint is set up about two miles up the highway from the station, to keep out nonessential personnel and people who want to gawk at our disaster driving in from Fairview. There is

The Deep End of Hope in the Wake of Hurricane Helene

Wi-Fi access at the checkpoint, and sometimes Jeff takes a shift manning it, so I go there to check in with him, since my phone still doesn't work.

I hitched a ride to our checkpoint earlier today in a bright, banana-colored Jeep Wrangler with a twelve-inch lift and forty-inch tires, so high off the ground I had to be helped into it. The Jeep was driven by a volunteer named Mitch, from Charlotte, who had been to many areas in NC over the past week. He said our community was the worst disaster he has seen.

I help Jeff to man the checkpoint for an hour. While I am there, our neighbors Sara and Pete show up with balloons, along with three young girls from our community, who have made a homemade birthday cake for Robert. Robert is a truck driver from Alabama who brought an emergency radio tower to extend the range of two-way radios for emergency workers, since still almost no one has cell phone service. He happened to have a Starlink in his truck, so that he could communicate and connect with the internet. He has graciously allowed community members access to his Wi-Fi. Robert sleeps in the truck, parked at the checkpoint, to monitor the equipment. Today is his birthday. We all sing to him.

Also at the checkpoint is a new-to-us neighbor, Robert, and his wife, Jean, who lovingly made a big pot of bear and chicken stew to share. Robert is a wild game hunter. They live up a mountain in our community, completely off-grid in the middle of a quiet forest.

The bear stew is really tasty. I never thought I would eat bear in my lifetime, but here we are.

Later, Jeff and I hitch a ride from the checkpoint to our fire station with former NC Representative John Ager, who tells us of some of the devastation in Black Mountain and Swannanoa, and the lack of water in Asheville, because reservoirs and miles of water pipes were destroyed.

I observed today that 95 percent of the people in our 300-person community are walking around open carry. Even women in their seventies and eighties are packing heat, due to looting and people getting squirrely because it really is the Wild West here on our mountain. It feels different here; it is this weird mix of feeling incredibly connected as a community but also very wary of what is happening around us.

We begin heading back up the mountain late this afternoon and discover North Carolina Department of Transportation (DOT) workers using rope to drop engineers wearing hard hats into the thirty-foot-deep chasm that was once the road connecting our HOA road to the highway. They are determining how to rebuild the giant hole into a road.

We see our neighbors Allison and Burt, who tell us that a military helicopter hovered twenty feet above their house, to do a wellness check. Someone in the helicopter peeked through the windows and asked for a thumbs-up or thumbs-down regarding status. They gave a thumbs-up.

Once home, we see that food and what would become ubiquitous water rations are waiting for us on our front porch (high protein rice and bean packets courtesy of Feed the Hunger in Burlington, NC).

We continue to spend every single night eating dinner with our neighbors, Erik and Kate, who both run missions each day to evacuate people and take food and (always) water supplies to remote communities. This is our opportunity to exchange news, to decompress, to work together to cook and clean up, and to have a sense of fellowship and normalcy, sometimes even with the lights on.

This is our favorite time of the day. This is what is helping us to make it through.

# Day 8 of the Apocalypse
Gerton, NC, Pop. ~~300~~ 301

Mary was thirty-eight weeks pregnant with her second child when Hurricane Helene devastated Gerton. In anticipation of the hurricane, her husband Jeremiah was convinced something horrendous would happen like mudslides and flooding.

Mary didn't believe him until the day before the hurricane when she saw someone post on Facebook, stating that the impact of Helene would be worse than the Great Flood of 1916. By the time Jeremiah got home from the grocery store Thursday afternoon, after stocking up on bread and milk, with dozens of other people waiting in the checkout lines, Mary was on board with Jeremiah's preparations.

They got bottles of water and flashlights ready and even went so far as to pack up Jeremiah's truck with provisions, a first aid kit, and walkie-talkies, in case they needed to evacuate quickly. Jeremiah is a former Marine and likes to be prepared. Jeff is the same way; preparing creates a sense of structure and safety. Preparing offers some level of comfort and hope, regardless of the outcome. Preparing makes the devastation more manageable.

They notified their closest neighbors, Katrina and Delia, as well as their family, of their plan. They asked Katrina if they could come to her house and make phone calls if the power went out, as Mary and Jeremiah rely on Wi-Fi calling.

Erik and another firefighter stopped by their house late Thursday afternoon, encouraging them to reach out to Erik if they needed help, because their house is only eight feet from a creek. Jeremiah and Mary decided, like almost all of us, to shelter in place. But they did ask Erik if they could come to his house if the water in their creek got too high. Erik lives closer to the top of the mountain and not near water.

Jeremiah reached out to their neighbor across the street, Delia, who has a waterfall behind her house, and told her that he was worried about landslides happening because of so much water. Jeremiah gave a walkie-talkie to Delia, in case she needed to reach them during the hurricane.

When Jeremiah and Mary woke up Friday morning, the creek started to rise considerably in just a matter of minutes. One minute it was a creek, and the next minute it was a flood, up to the first step of their porch.

They quickly packed a few more items of clothes, toothbrushes, phones, keys, and wallets, and got into their truck around 8:30 a.m. They attempted to drive up their steep driveway to the highway, but a giant tree was down across a big section, preventing them from turning left to head to the Gerton Fire Station, a mile away.

They tried turning right, to drive to the Bat Cave Fire Station, but another tree was down just a few yards away. They were trapped and couldn't get out. Jeremiah was still concerned about the possibility of landslides, especially because their house is down in a holler.

They decided to walk to their neighbor Katrina's house, about 400 meters away. Jeremiah carried their three-year-old son, Bill. Mary carried a backpack. They left their dogs in the house. In that moment they weren't thinking about the dogs; they were wondering if their family would make it out of this alive.

There was already a river of water coming across the road, up to Mary's ankles. She could feel the strength of the water trying to push her. They saw Katrina's house and the water and mud already surrounding it. They knew it was also a risk to stay at Katrina's, but they didn't feel like they could turn back. They made it to her house, arousing Katrina and her friend Sam, who invited them in.

Jeremiah went back to the house to get the dogs and a few more items, which terrified Mary. While he was inside of their house, the kitchen door flew open, and water and mud rushed into the house, from a landslide that has just occurred.

Jeremiah was able to barricade the door, but two and a half feet of sand, mud, and rocks came in before he could stop the damage. Their crawl space was flooded, and there were holes underneath the foundation, where water rushed in. Then another mudslide came down part of their driveway, carrying with it massive trees. Mary could hear these mudslides occurring from inside of Katrina's house down the road.

Somehow, Jeremiah managed to make it back to Katrina's with both dogs. Then he left again, this time to check on Delia on the other side of the highway, and to try and get her to the fire station. Mary knew he needed to go.

While he was gone, Mary heard another massive, rumbling mudslide. Bill was sitting on her lap, and Mary was comforting him, telling him that he would be safe. Katrina looked out her window, facing the highway, and her face went white. Mary started to freak out. Together they watched a gigantic tree rush by Katrina's house with Jeremiah still outside.

Mary felt, deep down, that he was okay. In retrospect, she doesn't know if she was fooling herself or just praying and believing that God was protecting Jeremiah. After about thirty minutes, Sam went out to try and find Jeremiah and Delia. Mary sat with Katrina and prayed, while Bill played with cars on the floor.

Finally, Sam came back and said, "I don't know if your neighbor Delia is still alive." Katrina burst into tears, but Mary refused to believe it.

She said, "No, Jeremiah and Delia are going to the fire station."

This time, Sam and Katrina left together in search of Jeremiah and Delia. Twenty minutes later the door opened and all four of them entered. Jeremiah and Delia were both soaking wet and fully covered in mud. Delia was in shock. A mudslide pushed her house off of its foundation. When Jeremiah saw her house, he too thought she was dead. He started screaming her name, and she finally popped her head out of a window. Jeremiah told her they had to leave. It took Delia a few minutes to register this. She evacuated through that same window, and they started walking to the fire station, less than a mile up the road.

They were walking through water and mud, up to their knees. They got about halfway up the road and saw multiple mudslides ahead of them, with others still happening around them. They turned back and went to Katrina's house, instead.

By midafternoon the rain stopped. Jeremiah and Delia attempted once more to get to the fire station. Assistant Chief Norris was there, cooking hot dogs on a small outdoor grill in the parking lot, and was happy to see them. Norris had been there all night and hadn't slept. The generator at the fire station wasn't working, so he had improvised by cooking on a grill, trying to feed people who began showing up continuously at the fire station, because even in the midst of devastation, you still have to remember to eat.

Some of those people were Airbnb guests, who didn't seem to understand what had just happened. Another community member there invited Delia to stay in his cottage. Jeremiah returned to Katrina's, and then he, Mary, their son, and their dogs returned to their own house.

They were delighted to discover that the mud inside didn't reach as far as their new-to-them sofa, which they had just been gifted by our mutual friend Linda. Mud was on the floor throughout the kitchen, bathroom, and part of the living room on the main level.

The three of them, exhausted, went upstairs to sleep, all piled into the same bed. Jeremiah didn't want Bill sleeping in a different room, in case there were more mudslides.

On Saturday, Day 2, they began discussing what to do if Mary started having contractions and went into labor. Katrina, who is a doula, offered to help. She had birthing materials in her house, because she had planned to help another pregnant woman give birth that same week. That baby was breech, though, so the woman was evacuated by helicopter from her house in Black Mountain.

Mary's due date was on October 13th, sixteen days away. She was going back and forth in her mind about whether to evacuate. Evacuation looked like hiking out with three-year-old Bill, bushwhacking through mud and downed trees. Staying meant being faced with no clean, potable water, and a house in major disrepair. She wasn't sure what was best for her, her baby, and her family.

Jeremiah vehemently wanted to stay in Gerton to help and to protect their property. If their property was vandalized or further damaged, there would be nowhere for them to live with the new baby. He also wanted Mary to stay and have a home birth with Katrina's help. That way, he could watch over his family and property at the same time.

Jeremiah's stance about staying made it hard for Mary to follow her maternal instincts to get out of dodge and to a fully functioning hospital to give birth. Mary and Jeremiah had different motivations in the wake of the disaster.

Two days later, on Monday, Day 4, paramedics showed up at their house. They somehow managed to trek through the Gorge, from Bat Cave. Jeremiah was at the fire station at the time. The man and woman offered to evacuate Mary immediately, because a helicopter was imminently scheduled to arrive at the Bat Cave campground, about a mile down the Gorge. They said the helicopter would take her to a hospital or somewhere else. She was terrified to make this decision on her own, knowing Jeremiah wanted them all to stay and for her to have a home birth. She was also scared to evacuate without him.

It is much easier to navigate a traumatic disaster when partners are on the same page about decisions. When they are not, it creates added stress and complications.

About thirty minutes later Jeremiah returned home, saw strange people in his driveway, and got very concerned about Mary and Bill. He was scared something had happened.

Once he knew why the paramedics were there, Jeremiah was in favor of Mary and their son evacuating to a hospital far enough away to have potable water, so she could give birth to their daughter there. But he felt he couldn't go with them.

Mary and their son left within fifteen minutes, taking with them a few newborn outfits, a baby blanket, and some clothes. Jeremiah gave them ear protection against the loud noise of the helicopter.

Mary, Bill, and the two paramedics hiked to the campground. They were only able to walk on the road for a small section, as most of it was covered in rubble. The majority of their walk was along a foot-wide path, hugging the mountain on one side, with a thirty-foot drop-off on the other side. One of the paramedics carried Bill through this.

They eventually made it to the campground, walking across the bridge that Erik and Jamie had made out of picnic tables. They were evacuated by basket, because there wasn't enough room for the helicopter to land.

In the basket, Mary reassured Bill that he was brave and was doing a great job. Mary recalls the basket spinning really fast the whole time it was being lifted into the helicopter. Bill was excited to be able to ride in the helicopter and gave high fives to National Guardsmen, once inside.

Once they landed, at East Henderson High School, one Henderson County worker took Mary and Bill to Advent Hospital, where her doctor works, so Mary could get checked out. Mary recalls driving through Hendersonville in shock, seeing almost no hurricane damage and lots of buildings and houses with power.

Mary was already two centimeters dilated and having contractions. But then they stopped, and a few hours later the hospital discharged her, with nowhere to go. Mary freaked out, but was able to reach her friend Emily, who had also evacuated. Emily found a place for her and Bill to stay overnight, and two other strangers to drive her to yet another stranger's house to sleep.

Somehow Mary ended up knocking on the wrong house when she and Bill were finally transported from the hospital at 11:00 p.m. She woke up the owner, who appeared in the doorway in a T-shirt and underwear, and remarkably invited them in to stay with her if needed. Mary declined and went two doors down to Fran's house. Fran looked like the little grandmother that everyone imagines having, and even had toys everywhere for Bill, as she often takes care of her grandkids. Mary felt relief.

In fact, Mary wasn't scared at all, after spending all day in the company of strangers. The only time she felt afraid was when the hospital discharged her, and she had no plan.

The next morning, Tuesday, Day 5, Emily picked Mary and Bill up and drove them to Charlotte, where Mary's sister then picked them up and drove them on to her home in Raleigh.

On Wednesday, Day 6, Mary got in touch with her insurance company for a list of OB doctors in Raleigh who were in network. She spent all day trying to get a doctor to accept her as a patient. Everyone said no; either they had no availability or wouldn't take Mary because she was already thirty-eight weeks pregnant.

Mary was on the phone so long and received so many nos that she ended up having a complete meltdown. She balled for a long time, not understanding why no one would help her. They didn't seem to comprehend that she had just been evacuated from her version of a war zone.

Eventually another friend got Mary in touch with a midwife, who agreed to work with her and have her admitted to a hospital only fifteen minutes from her sister's house. She made an appointment with the midwife for the following week.

That night, Jeremiah arrived at her sister's house, with their two dogs. Thirty-six hours later, on Friday morning, Day 8, Mary went into labor with immediate, big contractions. She and Jeremiah went to the hospital, leaving Bill in the care of her niece.

The hospital staff wasn't sure about admitting her, because they thought she was just in early labor. They asked if she wanted to be admitted or go back to her sister's house and wait. After seven days of too many hard decisions, Mary lost it. She started crying, so upset that her body went numb, and she couldn't feel her arms. The hospital staff empathized and admitted her, suggesting she take a nap and eat some food.

This is what happens when a person has been traumatized and is finally in a safe place. It is a complete breakdown. The ability to make decisions evaporates; the body refuses to cooperate.

Mary took a nap, and Jeremiah went out to get them Chick-fil-A, because that's what she ate when she was in labor with Bill and recalled loving it.

The labor was long and hard. The midwife told Mary it was because the baby was "sunny side up," meaning that she was head-first, but was facing upwards, which is what caused the days of on-again-off-again major contractions.

Mary believes that Allison came into this world all "scrambled up" from the spinning helicopter basket. She was born eight days early, in the middle of a devastated world.

Allison is a calm, easy baby.

# Day 9 of the Apocalypse
Gerton, NC, Pop. 301

Today was hard. The adrenaline rush of the hurricane is slowing down, and our residents are finally starting to respond emotionally to the disaster that struck us. When I was at the fire station for our daily community meeting, several people came up to me in tears, not knowing how to process their new reality.

I hugged Sara hard in the middle of the main road, surrounded by police cars, ATVs, residents, and dozens of volunteers. She hit a wall when her family ran out of propane for their generator this morning, and she cannot stop crying. Jeff brought her over to me as soon as he saw her. He isn't fond of women crying hysterically. I think it makes him nervous.

I consoled Matt, whose family isn't comprehending the state of the devastation and is telling him to just get over it. He is operating without water or power, and his road was destroyed. He's doing a phenomenal job of coping, but still berates himself for being so upset.

Shirley, a small, thin woman with a booming voice, arrived at the station hysterical. She feels unsafe with so many strangers using her property to get over the mountain. I sit on the pavement next to her, listening and holding space. She is still processing a rape from five years ago. The strangers are another form of violation to her.

Dave, an artist and trauma counselor, joins me on an abandoned trailer in a field. He is still in the midst of processing his own traumatic response to the destruction in our community, and in the River Arts District, and to his artwork. We swap stories about eerily similar childhood abuse, and for a moment I feel relief, knowing I am not alone in my multiple layers of devastation, of trauma on trauma.

I attended to a large, extended family, who tragically lost a two-year-old boy the day after the hurricane, when a gun accidentally went off.

This is complicated grief.

I lead our community, volunteers, and first responders in prayer. I remind everyone to be kind to themselves and compassionate with one another. I remind us that we are strong and that we will come out stronger on the other side of this.

Then my adrenaline starts slowing down, too. By midafternoon I have a raging migraine, the worst one I've had in probably a decade. Jeff and I are in Kate's car at the time. She left it parked at the fire station during the storm, and although water reached as high as the bottom of the car, no damage was done. The gas tank was almost on empty during the storm, so Jeff had requested via his "We are Gerton, NC" group that people drop off cans of gas, for this exact reason. The gas arrives, and we fill up her tank and borrow her car to go into town.

This is our first time out of Gerton. We drive to nearby Fairview, attempting to get groceries and ice and to pick up the mail. Our mail in Gerton has been rerouted to the Fairview Post Office, because our post office flooded from the creek directly behind it. There is a lot of mail waiting for us, including some beautiful care packages of electrolytes from colleagues and clients and bills for services we no longer have, like electricity and internet.

It is upsetting to be only eight miles away from home, and to see people out mowing their lawns, when we don't even have roads. I notice myself getting angry at them. *What right do they have to operate lawn mowers at a time like this? Who are they to complain about anything when they have power and cell phone service?*

I want to scream at them. My migraine is worsening. I feel like vomiting. Jeff is angry, too; I can tell. Everything we are seeing sets him on edge. The lights in the grocery store are too bright. There are too many people driving around. Folks are pumping gas into their cars like it is no big deal. Some of them even dare to stand in line at the post office to mail packages.

In my mind, I shout, *How can people be doing these things when there are dead bodies just down the road from here?* Search and rescue is still going on in Bat Cave and Chimney Rock. Multiple people have told us that as many as 300 people are still missing.

Most of Fairview is still without water. No one knows how long it will take for that to be restored. These people are having their own version of the apocalypse. It just happens to look radically different from ours. That doesn't make their pain less than ours.

There is no hierarchy of suffering.

We return to the Gerton Fire Station as quickly as possible, and I hurry inside because I think I am having a medical emergency with my roaring head pain. Fire Chief Jay comes and checks on me, and Assistant Fire Chief Norris sits next to me and holds my hand. Norris starts telling me funny stories, trying to divert my attention from the pounding in my head. I've been working as a team member with these men, and it is so thoughtful of them to take a break in the middle of their very stressful responsibilities to attend to me.

Mainly, I just want someone to shove a giant ice pick into the back of my head, to relieve the pressure and pain. I wonder to myself how to find an ice pick during an apocalypse and who I could ask to assist me. I am not feeling suicidal; I just need relief.

Jay and Norris bring over Dylan, a Tom-Cruise-level, ripped, tanned, shirtless cardiac nurse in his sixties, to check my vitals. I'm not sure if they are trying to distract me from my pain, or if Dylan is the only medical professional available. (No, no one knows why the hell Dylan is shirtless.)

Dylan checks my vitals, and everything seems normal. That's the thing about migraines. The person having them is the only one who can tell there is suffering. I've been getting migraines since I was eleven. Then, it was a coping mechanism for me. It was unsafe to have feelings or needs in my family. Now, it is still a coping mechanism; my body tells me when I am doing too much or pushing myself too far.

My chronic Lyme disease flares up when I am under stress or when I do too much physically. It shows up as all over inflammation, which makes every part of my body hurt. I also experience brain fog and headaches, which make me cranky and hard to be around.

This past week has been nonstop stress. We are continually operating in the unknown with things changing minute-by-minute. I've been pushing my body to its limits, on the go for twelve to fourteen hours a day. There is so much to do to keep our household operational with limited generator power. Every day, I'm checking on neighbors or their houses and hiking down to the fire station to serve as trauma chaplain. I'm still struggling to sleep through the night.

My hips hurt. My calves ache. My back is sore. My legs are covered in bruises from bushwhacking and hauling supplies around. I'm frustrated with my body and my mind. Can't they both see that I need them to keep up because there is so much to do every day?

Dylan tells me I need to take a break from the chaos. And today was many hours of constant chaos. I know he is right.

Tim, one of our local firefighters, takes me up the mountain in an ATV to our house. He's been sleeping at the firehouse because his home is on the other side of the mountain, and what used to be a twenty-five-minute commute now takes one-and-a-half hours via a circuitous route.

Once home, I take a nap and sleep hard. The migraine passes, but the apocalypse remains.

# Day 10 of the Apocalypse
Gerton, NC, Pop. 301

Today is a rest day for me after overdoing it with the migraine yesterday. Plus, we decided that it would be good for one of us to stay on the mountain in case a helicopter arrives to evacuate Paul and Susan. We want to be able to help them get to the helicopter.

I'm at home, alone for the first time in eight days. It is dark and chilly in our house. Even though the sun is out, it's too early in the day for it to be streaming through our windows. The house is eerily quiet. It's creeping me out a bit to be here by myself. Erik, Kate, and Jeff are all down the mountain.

Our HOA cattle gate is permanently open. It was originally opened for emergency personnel, but now that access has been extended to a myriad of volunteers. Anyone can come up at any time, by ATV at least, and I have no way to get ahold of help. We have had looters from within our community as well as people coming in from other areas, trying to take supplies, everything from food to heavy equipment. County officials initiated a curfew a few nights ago because of this. It is their way of trying to stop people from moving around at night in the cover of darkness. Everyone around here is armed, and I am not. I have to remind myself that fear is a choice.

Before he left this morning, Jeff wanted to show me how to operate a gun, in case I needed to protect myself. I refused to touch it, as if holding it would cause violence to erupt. I am one of the few in Gerton who doesn't have a weapon on them. Until today, I've always been near other people who could protect me if something happened.

Alone in the house, the only sounds I can hear are the constant churn of helicopter rotor blades flying directly above our house. Chinook, Black Hawk, Bell JetRanger, National Guard, medical, private. All types are out today.

I'm used to always asking Jeff to turn down the television during the day. My office is right next to our living room, and I can hear the TV when I am sitting at my desk, even with the door closed. The noise makes it hard for me to concentrate. Now I don't even *want* to think.

I don't want to reflect on my feelings about the devastation. They are not particularly helpful or useful right now. I have noticed though that I haven't been able to care about anything outside of Gerton, even about Hurricane Milton, which is threatening to blast the west coast of Florida any day now. Even news from other parts of Western North Carolina feels irrelevant.

Other devastation isn't my devastation. I can only hold so much.

What little I have seen on Facebook, of things happening in other parts of reality, has irritated me. It's hard for me to be joyous about someone else's vacation photos or thriving business or new outfit.

I feel like an asshole.

I don't even care that I feel like an asshole. I just want to shout from the rooftops, "What is wrong with you people? How can you carry on as if this is not happening?"

It is a slap-in-the-face recognition that unless *you* are living it, there is no way to truly understand. This lack of understanding will only get worse when the Helene news cycle is over.

People from my outside world run the gamut between asking me if I've recovered yet, to suggesting that I'll never be able to recover without intensive therapy. Others are hoping that I'll still be able to vote in the upcoming election, like I can even think about something like that right now. I know their comments are well meaning, but I hate them. I don't want to respond. There is no true recovery. I am already recovered, as much as I can be. There is no answer I can give that feels accurate, because I don't fucking know how I am doing.

There is no luxury of self-care or reflection in the midst of just trying to get basic needs met.

I spend the morning cleaning up around the house. Then I walk up the road to our neighbors Bobby and Meredith's house, because when I stand on their back porch and hold up my phone, I can sometimes get cell signal. I've been trying for days to apply for FEMA disaster relief. We already suspect that all we've get from FEMA is an initial $750 to cover the loss of food, but this gives me a sense of purpose and is something I can do to improve our situation. But because cell signal is so spotty for me, I can never get all of the way through the process.

Each time I log into the FEMA app, I have to enter a security code that gets sent via text to my phone. This is an extra protective step to ensure no one else can access my account. My cell signal isn't strong enough to receive text messages or comment on Facebook posts or look up things on the internet. I am only able to use the FEMA app, and post things to Facebook. So, no security code for me today.

Every person's cell phone signal is a little different. Jeff is able to receive and send texts, comment on Facebook, and look up things on the internet. The internet has only been available to him for a few days. Texting was available by Day 3.

Each day I dutifully walk to a location with stronger signal than our house and try to apply for disaster relief, hoping that maybe one day I'll see the security code come through. I still haven't been able to have a conversation with anyone in the outside world. Even if I were to get strong enough signal, I'm not sure I would know what to say. How would I summarize this new reality?

After a while ATVs start showing up in our neighborhood. Yesterday was the first day we saw ATVs up here, as a path was finally cut for them up our road. The first one that arrived carried Ben, Paul and Susan's son, who traveled here from Charleston to evacuate them. He originally intended to help them evacuate by helicopter, and then hike out himself, but now that's no longer necessary. We have ATV access! I ran down the road, eager to celebrate this news, and hugged the guys who brought Ben up the mountain.

This morning Kate drove up in a big side-by-side to evacuate Paul, Susan, Ben, and their dog and cat down the mountain. It was fun seeing our octogenarian former HOA president riding in the back of the UTV. He, like all of us, is just doing what needs to be done.

The first UTV has small tanks of propane to distribute (like the ones people use for outdoor grills). The second has cases and cases of bottled water. The third has five guys spilling out of it. They are going door to door assessing damage, at the request of our fire chief. The UTVs are all full of men. I am alone on the mountain. There is no way for me to get ahold of Jeff if I need help. The only recourse is to assume that I am safe.

"God, protect me. Encircle me in Love. Ensure that no harm comes to me." But I do take note of the gun sitting on our dining room table, which gives me no comfort.

I take the last group of strange men to Paul and Susan's house, which has a giant chestnut tree leaning over it, poised to topple. Although we got them evacuated, we still want to ensure their home doesn't sustain further damage.

Enroute home from their house, I see a black bear cross the road about ten feet in front of me. I am so excited to see him—a first since the hurricane—that I start talking to him, just like I do my dogs.

"Hey, Mr. Bear! How are you doing? Are you having a good day today? Look at how handsome you are! You're so furry. What a good bear! What are you doing today? Are you going for walkies?"

Mr. Bear is not amused. Apparently, I am blocking his egress, causing a traffic jam. So I get out of his way, and he continues his mission.

A couple of hours later, Shawn, a.k.a. "Animal" shows up in a fluorescent yellow, giant ATV. Animal is a stucco mason from Chattanooga, TN, with a foot-long, white, braided goatee and a gigantic smile. He uses his massive chainsaw to start clearing the trees from our road by himself. This will allow us to get vehicles out of our driveways and down our shared road. Jeff gave him a Gerton T-shirt to thank him for his service, which he now wears daily.

Animal volunteers regularly in disaster zones, sleeping in a camper that he hand built for his truck. He said he loves being able to get to know new people and support others in this way. For a moment, I am soothed by his presence and service.

This is what apocalyptic Love looks like in action.

# Reflections on Trauma in the Rescue Phase

The American Psychological Association defines trauma as "an emotional response to a terrible event like an accident, crime, or natural disaster."[5] Trauma can also be characterized not by the event itself, but by one's reaction to it. Peter Levine, a well-known psychological trauma theorist, explains that any overwhelming and distressing experience can cause trauma. He believes that trauma is only recognizable by its symptoms.

In the rescue phase, the immediate aftermath, shock and disbelief are often the first symptoms, followed closely by numbness or denial. Emotions that follow are often high levels of anxiety, guilt, or depression, similar to the stages of grief.

When basic needs are not met, it is virtually impossible to pay attention to or attend to the emotional symptoms of trauma. When there is no shelter, food, rest, or safety, the last thing anyone is capable of is having feelings or experiencing them.

---

[5] https://www.apa.org/topics/trauma

That is a normal response in the wake of a traumatic event. There is nothing wrong with that. Attending to trauma at this time becomes a series of simple questions to dissipate shock and disbelief:

> Do you have shelter?
>
> Do you have food?
>
> Do you need medical support?
>
> Are you physically safe?
>
> Are you sleeping?

These were the questions I asked our community members during the rescue phase, those first ten days following the hurricane. The focus at this time needs to be on safety and stabilization.

Those of us who came together in the devastation spent the first ten days repeating our stories to one another. There was catharsis in this. Being able to share these stories and speak with others who had gone through something similar, helped us to reframe and make sense of what had happened. It allowed us to not feel so alone or helpless.

Some of us, strangers before Helene, created significant bonds in a very short amount of time. There are men and women in our community who I didn't know before, who I now consider brothers and sisters. My family has multiplied ten times over.

When Mary finally lost it emotionally on Day 8, that was the first time she felt safe enough and sheltered enough to have a visceral response to the trauma she experienced.

Some people evacuated sooner than Mary did, and their emotional response started immediately. Many experienced anxiety and guilt around leaving.

A former client of mine (I am a spiritual advisor and mentor) who also lives in Asheville spoke about feeling overwhelmed and frozen by sadness, having evacuated to another state a few days after the hurricane. She called herself "one of the lucky ones," because her home didn't sustain damage, and she was able to evacuate. In the next breath, she expressed guilt for having left, instead of staying to help. "Being fortunate" is intertwined with grief over those who lost so much more than she did. Helping herself is confused with guilt over leaving.

This survivor's guilt is all-pervasive and also a trauma response. That was often the first thing I heard, when attending to people as a chaplain. "My home is gone, but so many other people are worse off than I am."

There is no hierarchy of suffering. Pain does not need to be measured alongside someone else's.

There is no "right" amount of suffering, or pain, to justify how we are responding or feeling. There is no "right" way to respond. There is only how we choose to show up in each moment.

As I shared earlier, challenge can make us bitter or better. We have the choice in each moment how we want to feel about what we are facing. Other people can also help us to navigate this choice.

In the rescue phase, other people showing up in apocalyptic Love can help those of us living in the midst of devastation to heal. Their love shines on us, giving us hope and offering us comfort.

During the rescue phase, here is the prayer I wished upon all those who I sat with:

> Breathe into the shelter that is offered to you.
> 
> Breathe into the meals placed before you
> 
> Breathe into the warmth that surrounds you.
> 
> Keep breathing it all in.
> 
> Breathing in, then out, is your spiritual practice right now.
> 
> And that is enough.
> 
> You are held. You are carried. You are loved.

# PART 2
# RECOVERY

## Day 11 of the Apocalypse
Gerton, NC, Pop. 301

We are ground zero.

I didn't understand until today that the Hickory Nut Gorge, comprising (from north to south) Gerton, Bat Cave, Chimney Rock, and Lake Lure, was one of the hardest hit during Helene.

Somehow the weather system stalled right above our Gorge Friday morning, September 27th, which is what caused the massive flooding and microbursts that caused trees to collapse. A microburst is a localized column of sinking air within a storm. Similar to a downdraft, and often confused with a tornado, microbursts can cause extensive damage.

Our friends Stan and Dave, for example, had dozens of trees, mainly large poplars, cover their mile-long road. They were hit by a microburst.

Now I get why we've had so many volunteers and donations show up.

As of today, we've asked people to stop bringing general donations and unskilled volunteer support to Gerton. We are full for now with supplies, including a mountain of bottled water, diapers, and baby formula. We only have two babies in Gerton, and we have enough baby supplies to stock an entire city of babies. We have thankfully run out of things for unskilled labor to do.

It is getting cold. We need winter supplies now like camp stoves, heaters, winter jackets, and generators. We also need specialty items, like Starlink systems and carbon monoxide detectors for homes that are running propane heaters inside.

Jeff is meeting several people today who are dropping off key supplies like Starlink systems for our community to have Wi-Fi access, as well as one hundred gallons of gas. The gas will refuel all of the ATVs being used to make supply deliveries to remote areas of our fire district. Erik and Kate are continuing rescue missions. It's just a typical day now. Everyone has their assigned tasks and are executing them.

Our fire station is full to the brim with too many supplies and volunteers, which is so different from just a week ago when there were only four people running rescue missions and no supplies. Erin, who is married to firefighter Jacob, has been organizing the supplies. She's an exceptional organizer. Piles are neatly put together by category. Food and essentials are lined up in the back of the station, in front of the gear for the firefighters. Baby supplies and feminine hygiene products are in the back room. The overwhelming amount of donated water bottles has been moved to the back bay.

I have taken to grabbing eight-ounce containers of protein drinks out of the supply piles to get enough protein into my system. It's too hard to eat solid food when I'm down at the fire station. There's too much going on. I am attending to people who are devastated. Eating feels hard.

We will need supplies again probably in a couple of weeks. Jeff continues to coordinate with our fire department and the outside world regarding urgent needs. We are in it for the long haul with having no power or internet signal.

We have an urgent need for skilled labor: sawyers (people who use chainsaws professionally) with technical skills to cut giant trees; crane operators to help the sawyers; road reconstruction crews; home restoration experts, as mold is forming in houses that were flooded;

and, of course, lineworkers to replace all of our downed power lines and restore electricity to our area.

Gerton is now officially in the recovery phase.

Bat Cave, Chimney Rock, and Lake Lure (where parts of *Dirty Dancing* was filmed) remain in the rescue phase. We hear that hundreds of people are still missing.

Searching for people is complicated because the road between Gerton and these communities is gone. It is now a giant pile of rocks, debris, and washed away homes. This was caused by Hickory Creek, and the Rocky Broad River, which both used to run next to the highway, overtaking the road during the storm. The water extended itself by forty to a hundred feet, washing out all bridges, all adjacent houses, businesses, and the highway.

There is no way to easily maneuver around these communities to search for bodies. Skilled rescue workers are working diligently to clear debris and rubble to find people. Cadaver dogs are on site. Some ATV paths have been made to help get rescue workers into more remote areas. Cell service is still limited, hindering efforts to find people.

Erik has been a part of searching for missing people and bodies in Gerton and Bat Cave. He is one of two rescue technicians in our fire department, and the only one who has previous experience with finding dead bodies. He selflessly offered to go when he was called on to help, because he wanted to protect those in his department who had not already been exposed to this horrendous work.

NCDOT called on Erik to search an area of the highway between Gerton and Bat Cave that was overtaken by a mudslide. Erik, DOT, and state troopers were all on scene. State troopers were onsite because if there is a fatality on or near a road, they are responsible for that fatality. However, it is not their job to do rescues; this work falls to rescue technicians. So Erik was the one actively searching, while DOT and the state troopers assisted where they could.

There was a car that has been caught in the mudslide. Erik knows the owner and her children, and they haven't been found yet. There was a possibility that he might find them in the car, which was flipped upside down and covered in mud, preventing anyone from being able to look inside.

Erik ended up using an electric saw to cut a hole through the bottom of the car, to see if people were inside. This was arduous work, and at one point Erik leaned back to take a break, resting his hand in the mudslide. He inadvertently touched a buried dead chicken, which "popped," immediately exploding releasing a nauseating gas and covering Erik in chicken debris. This wasn't the first time he encountered dead animals in his searches. To date, he's found a horse and two deer, either in mudslides or caught in the riverbanks.

Tonight, as Erik's telling us this story, he's recollecting that the combined smell of flesh, fuel, and mud now causes a trauma response in him. He instinctively gags and recoils.

Here's the worst part of this story. Erik, Kate, Jeff, and I are sitting, per usual, on our L-shaped living room sofa. Really, it's the three of them sitting on the sofa, and me, lying on the floor with the dogs eagerly licking my face, while I'm trying to stretch out my back. Our battery-powered lamp is on the ottoman between us, offering a little light in the midst of total darkness.

Erik is eager to tell us this story. I can tell he's had a really challenging day, and he needs to debrief what has happened. This is what we do late at night; we each debrief our days. This is our unspoken agreement. This is how we are making it through this, together. Today was hard core rescue and recovery work that Erik is still doing, on Day 11.

But Kate and I don't want to hear the story. We are exhausted. Our adrenaline has disappeared. Erik's has not. He's still super hyped up, really in his element. The apocalypse represents everything he has ever trained for as a firefighter and rescue technician. He's still jumping out of bed each morning, eager to start the day. He is putting himself in incredibly precarious positions to help friends and strangers who live in our fire district.

Erik will not rest until the job is finished. In fact, he's literally not sleeping, like many others in our community. They want to ensure that everyone is accounted for and safe. Some community members believe they will personally rescue and recover all of Gerton and don't seem to want anyone else here helping us out.

I don't know if it's extreme enthusiasm or protecting what has already been accomplished in the first week, which—let's be honest here—is stunning and miraculous. Few people, in a very short amount of time, were able to assess all 300 of our residents, and assure their safety, without anyone else coming in to help.

By the beginning of week two, there was a ton of outside help, including other first responders. A professional government search and rescue team arrived, attempting to take over, but everyone in our community was already accounted for, and all areas had already been searched, multiple times.

Samaritan's Purse came in with an ER doctor and RNs, who rode around on side-by-sides attempting to do wellness checks on people who had already been evacuated because of their medical conditions or checking on people who had already been checked on multiple times. They came to my house, and I remember being irritated that someone I didn't know was coming up on my property and wanting to give me something I hadn't asked for.

There was a particularly obnoxious guy named Darrell, who rolled up to our fire department in a jacked-up UTV, ready to "save Gerton." He was a blogger, who was committed to "taking care of us" and "praying for us" because he knew it was "too hard for us to do anything right now." He stayed for a week, creating his own missions to "help you poor people."

These outsiders want to come in and take credit for rescue efforts, but they don't seem willing to do the hard things that our community members have done without blinking. Within the first five days, every person in Gerton was accounted for. By the end of the second week all our main roads will be accessible, and all private roads will be free of downed trees and temporarily cleared. The majority of this worked happened without outside help.

There is an historical mistrust that Appalachian people have of others coming in to help. We saw this play out in several ways. For example, people who retired here from Florida or other states would constantly ask our fire department to check in with those "poor people" that lived near them, not understanding that these mountain people, who have lived here for generations, were doing perfectly well in the wake of this historical catastrophe. But because the mountain people had fewer means than those who relocated here, it was assumed they needed help.

There are people who *do* need help, who are still missing, whose houses were washed away. There is a Hurricane Safety Check-In group on Facebook, where people have been posting photos of their family members with addresses of where they live, desperately asking for any information about whether they are alive.

Here's an example of a post: "Please help us find ____ who lives in Chimney Rock, NC. We spoke with her right before the hurricane. We think her home was destroyed and have filed a missing persons' report."

The comments and responses on this particular post are surreal:

"We cut our way into Lake Lure and Chimney Rock this morning. The damage is unimaginable. After abandoning their boat, three of our rescue swimmers were able to swim across the river to reach Chimney Rock. Our team was the first one from outside the village to reach Chimney Rock Fire Department and began assisting with rescues and evacuations. We successfully made 252 contacts of persons, rescued four souls who are doing well and one pup; we evacuated 106 souls, two dogs, and two cats. Our NC System is strong. No electronics, no cells, very little radio, and everyone pulled together today including our state and military aircraft, often without contact or instructions. We are back at it tomorrow."

"I friended her family on Facebook and asked for a status. Someone was able to reach her thru her daughter's phone."

"There is a post on one of her Facebook pages that's not good news. It appears that the fire department went to rescue her, but she refused to go because her dog could not be found. Shortly thereafter her house was swept away, and she is missing."

"I've just learned that the Rutherford County Sheriff's Department and the FBI have contacted the family and are actively searching her cell phone records."

"God, help them locate her."

A few days later this comment was made: "Her family announced today that she did not make it. Asking for private time."

We are on Day 11, and there is still so much more to be done.

Our prayers are with everyone affected by Helene, but especially here in our Gorge.

# Day 12 of the Apocalypse
## Ground Zero, Gerton, NC, Pop. 301

I made the incredibly difficult decision to put all of my private mentoring with clients on hold until the beginning of January.

This was agonizing for me, because I love working with my clients, and I'm helping many of them with projects that are quite time sensitive. The good girl in me wants to be able to do everything, to somehow magically be able to run my business even though we still don't have power, we're still rationing propane, and I still don't have cell service strong enough for phone calls. The scared girl in me is terrified that my clients will leave and that my business will fail if I don't keep working on it every day.

The part of me that has remarkably strong access to my intuition right now keeps telling me that I need to keep my focus here. After several conversations with Jeff, we recognize that both our hearts are with our local community right now, Jeff serving as the supply coordinator and chief communicator via his Gerton Facebook group, and me serving as the trauma chaplain. This is how we *want* to be spending our time. This is a once-in-a-lifetime event, and we want to be boots on the ground here.

To be honest, it's also hard to think about anything outside of Gerton. I scroll through Facebook and see people posting about things that irritate me: marketing for Thanksgiving or Christmas; calls to action from my colleagues running businesses; people sharing photos of trips they are on; funny dog memes. I can't get myself to care about anything.

We went to Fairview again a few days ago. We used Kate's car again, which remains parked at the fire station. There is power and internet there, although still no water. We picked up a few items at the grocery store, along with five big bags of ice. We need the ice now to keep food cold enough, as we are running the generator for only three or four hours a day to conserve our propane, which is down to 18 percent as of today. The meter on our propane tank indicates that we have officially hit the red zone.

We check our post office box, put gas in the car, and have normal conversations with people about the weather and other things that don't matter to me anymore. It still completely stresses me out. I can't be normal right now when people are still missing and our neighbors have lost their homes.

I think that is part of my trauma response.

I've also lost the ability to multitask or remember anything. Jeff and I have taken to writing everything down on Post-it notes, so we don't forget.

We call them "Post-it Notes from the Edge." They are mainly lists like this:

*Protein drinks*

*Chainsaw oil*

*Find Dave*

*Tiny houses*

*Check on Amy*

*Propane delivery?*

Reminders of the things we need to do once we get down to the fire station, because it's such an ordeal to get back up the mountain. We have to plan out every day to maximize our limited energy and access to resources. Jeff and I are both so tired. We're in our fifties and aren't used to hiking down and up a mountain every day. Oftentimes, we can find someone with a side-by-side to drive us and our supplies up. But it's still exhausting to spend all day, every day, focusing on getting our basic needs met, all while spending most of the day on our feet. Everything must be planned out and timed. Everything requires physical effort. Every. Single. Thing.

We spend a lot of time repeating things to each other, because we're also unable to take in information very easily. It's wild how our trauma response is manifesting. A lot of people are getting really angry or sad. Jeff and I experience it most when we can't get our brains to work. Sometimes we're quick to snap at each other, "You told me that five minutes ago!" Other times, we are too tired to snap, we just listen, and we don't retain most of what is said.

Jeff's current project is to create a mobile hotspot for people in remote areas of our community, to be able to use the internet and make phone calls. He's gotten a Starlink system, and a small generator donated, a combined value of nearly $1,000. Most people in our area still have intermittent cell service and either no internet or no ability to access the internet service they do have without power. Jeff wants to be able to travel throughout our fire district to get internet access to those people who aren't able to get to the fire station or out of Gerton. We're on Day 12 and many people still haven't been able to contact their loved ones or their insurance companies or apply for FEMA disaster relief.

## Day 13 of the Apocalypse
### Ground Zero, Gerton, NC, Pop. 301

We had some HUGE wins today! And y'all, I NEEDED some wins.

First, Blossman Gas, our propane delivery service, somehow by the grace of God found a way to get to our house to deliver propane. We were down to 15 percent by the time they arrived.

Last night I had a meltdown with Jeff, thinking that on top of everything else going on, we were also about to lose precious access to our whole house generator power for a few hours a day.

The meltdown went from crying and feeling sorry for myself to getting frustrated at my husband for prioritizing helping, you know, our ENTIRE community instead of me. Jeff spends four to six hours a day coordinating supplies, and the rest of his sixteen-hour days relaying critical information to the outside world.

I feel like I'm never going to be normal again.

Jeff, who is from New Orleans and lived through Hurricane Katrina, calmly told me that I will never be the same again and that this once-in-1,000-year hurricane event will change the trajectory of my life forever. He said it with the same tone he uses when asking me to pass the salt.

The problem is that Jeff is always right.

We are facing war against an apocalypse, and his fierce love is the only consolation he can offer me right now. We choose what horror teaches us. Jeff's experience with natural disasters, having lived in New Orleans for fifty years, taught him to harden his heart and do what needs to be done in the face of disaster. He's showing me that my tender heart won't make it through.

I hug Josh, the delivery man/rock star propane truck driver, hard. He pulled up to our house, just like it was a regular delivery day and like what he was doing was completely normal. He seemed surprised by how shocked and thrilled we were to see him.

He said he has fourteen more deliveries after ours, spanning 204 miles, since so many roads are blocked. Josh works seven 12-hour days in a row right now, in order to keep on top of post-hurricane demand. He says that he's getting lots of hugs from people like me, and he knows the work he's doing is invaluable. Josh also said it's hard for him to not get home in time to tuck his three-year-old daughter into bed.

I ask Josh if he would fill our first responder, next door neighbor's tank, even though they are not Blossman customers, and add their propane to our bill. He agreed!

This is especially significant because our internet signal is beamed from their house, which has clear line of sight to the Skyrunner antennae on top of Little Pisgah Mountain. In order to access internet, both of our generators need to be running. So now we know that we can check things online, every morning and evening, and that our good friends will still be able to have power in their home, too.

With internet access, Jeff can continue to coordinate supplies being delivered from the outside, and I can work on our FEMA application, my Small Business Administration Economic Disaster Injury application (which is ridiculously long), and pay our Duke Energy bill, even though we haven't had power for almost two weeks.

Jeff and I were able to drive his truck down to the bottom of our road so that we only had to hike a mile to the fire station.

We discover that the road that connects our HOA road to the highway, which was a thirty-foot-deep chasm a week ago, will be drivable by tomorrow for trucks and ATVs.

Here's how we discovered that. Jeff saw a woman from a private construction company standing in the middle of the chasm. Well, he didn't see her at first. He was loading up the back of his truck with two generators, a Starlink for us, and three cans of gas to power the generators. He saw the top of her head. Then it disappeared. Then he noticed it again when she started shouting at him.

He walked over and peered into the cavern. The woman said, "Is where I am standing a road?" She had been sent by her company to oversee the road reconstruction. Jeff let her know that she was in the right place. Then he asked her how long it would take to construct the road, and she said, "By tomorrow." Jeff's jaw dropped, stunned that the road could be fixed so quickly.

This road is a lifeline for everyone on our mountain, and it's a big deal that we're going to be able to get trucks up and down it.

The ATV path along this road, on our friends Patrick's and Sharon's properties, is a muddy, treacherous mess. At one point, the ATVs have to drive essentially sideways along a steep hill. Everyone in the ATV must lean over to one side to keep it from tipping over. It's also important to keep shoulders and hands way inside the ATV, to keep free of the branches.

Patrick has constant traffic right next to his house, impacting his wife, child, and three golden retrievers. It will be good for his family to get some semblance of normalcy again.

Another win: A Baptist pastor gave me a compliment. His church is running a food truck in the parking lot of our fire station, serving hot meals daily from 11 a.m.-5 p.m. for community members and first responders.

I'm used to being ignored by male Baptist pastors in Appalachia, because a lot of them won't acknowledge women as ministers. He complimented me on the prayer I gave at the community meeting, saying it was just what people needed to hear. This was huge for me, because I know I look and talk different from most of the people I am ministering to.

David, the pastor, also reminded me of the importance of listening to God's calling during times like this when things may not go as expected.

David is right, and I'm so grateful that he blessed me with his ministry. I needed a reminder that I am in exactly the right place at this time, that this is all happening *for* me, and that I am in fact open and able to hear guidance about my next steps.

David's ministry is for everyone, friends.

# Day 14 of the Apocalypse
## Ground Zero, Gerton, NC, Pop. 301

Instead of burying the lead, let me share that Jeff's recent request for a Starlink system for his mobile hotspot was sent by a friend of a friend to Elon Musk's mother, Maye.

Starlink is an advanced satellite technology that delivers high-speed internet and was developed by Elon Musk. The retail price of a Starlink ranges from $300-$700.

The Starlink system looks like a white pizza box with a kickstand to be set up in an open area outside (i.e., not under trees and facing north). It requires power, but only as much as is needed to power a lamp. Once powered, the pizza box uses its own technology to track satellites in the sky (which are constantly in motion) and jumps between their signals to deliver steady internet. It's a lightweight miracle connection to the world.

The best part is that when connected to a generator, a Starlink offers great Wi-Fi anywhere in our fire district. Elon Musk offered all hurricane victims free access to Starlink through the end of this year. Service is normally around $120 a month. For people in our area who have lost jobs and homes, this is an extremely generous gift.

Elon Musk is literally Jeff's favorite person right now, because his Starlink technology is the only thing that has allowed Gerton community members to have contact with the outside world post-Helene.

We got ours yesterday and it will now be easier for Jeff to communicate with the outside world. We also hope this Wi-Fi connection will enable my cell phone to work. The Starlink is sitting on top of a picnic bench, which is placed on top of our picnic table outside of my office window. Jeff covered the picnic table with a tarp, so the Wi-Fi router of the Starlink situated underneath the table remains dry if it starts raining. We're powering our Starlink with a small gas generator, which is parked out back beside our bedroom door.

We have a second generator on our front porch, which is plugged into the television, by way of a long orange extension cord through our living room window. Jeff set this up so at night, when we turn off our generator, he, Erik, Kate, and I can watch movies. We're still sitting in the dark, but now the television is on, which is a welcome distraction and respite.

Jeff is also attempting to secure additional Starlink systems for people who live in clusters of homes. His vision is to install a Starlink at a house that is close to several others, enabling everyone in that area to have Wi-Fi access. I know I sound like a commercial for Elon Musk, but the impact that having internet has had during this period is invaluable.

In other news, Jeff and I made a big decision to draw from our savings and purchase a new Kubota UTV to help us navigate getting up and down our mountain and around Gerton.

A utility terrain vehicle, a.k.a. UTV or side-by-side vehicle (often just called a side-by-side), is a compact, four-wheel-drive, gas-powered vehicle with a side-by-side seating arrangement. Ours has a bench seat up front for two people as well as a big cargo bed in the back for hauling around supplies, or, if needed, other people. UTVs are designed for work, not recreation like golf carts are. The UTV is a more advanced version of an ATV, which typically has a straddle seating position and almost no space for hauling anything other than one or two people.

We purchased the UTV because we recognize that it could be months before we have power and properly reconstructed roads. All roads from our house to the fire station are now technically drivable, dependent on no heavy rain causing more mudslides and driving under five miles an hour, and as long as there is no electricity shooting through fallen power lines above and below us.

Yesterday we drove Jeff's truck down our HOA road and the second road (now open) that connects our road to the highway. We both agreed it was a terrifying experience. Mainly I kept my eyes closed and listened to Jeff gasp and curse as he navigated the narrow, treacherous path with no place to pull over if another car had tried to pass by us.

The UTV works best for our new reality. So, I'm going to be a side-by-side driver. Add that to my list of things I never thought I would be or do.

A new friend, Sean, saw Jeff's post about needing help sourcing a UTV. He called around to find one in our area that could be delivered quickly. Because of his good efforts, we were able to get to a dealer yesterday and make a quick purchase.

The side-by-side will assist Jeff's efforts to get a mobile Starlink hooked up to a generator in the remote areas of our fire district, so people there can have access to phone and internet. I will travel with him to offer trauma chaplain services for people who can't get to the fire station.

We didn't really want to spend this kind of money, but we knew it was the right decision for our needs as well as for helping meet the needs of our community.

We work with Logan at Kubota of Asheville, a family-run business. Logan has worked at his family's dealership since high school. He performs miracles to get us a great price and is ensuring that we are number one in line for delivery because he wants to do his part in supporting Gerton, too.

Enroute home we stop by Ansley's house (another new friend) in Asheville and pick up a brand-new Generac Generator that she wants to donate to Gerton.

We also drive to Market Street in Asheville, which looks pristine but deserted. Jeff is getting some key supplies from AVL F.A.S.T., which stands for Asheville Friends Assisting Survivors Together. They are gathering supplies in a place called The Venue, which normally operates as a wedding venue. The facility is filled with young hipster types, full of energy that we no longer have. We load up Jeff's truck with four Starlink systems, along with lots of other supplies that volunteers put in the truck once they realized we were from Gerton. I think we are the first people from the Hickory Nut Gorge that they have seen.

It continues to amaze me how many people are stepping up. Every time we ask for support someone says yes, usually within twenty-four hours. We deeply feel all the ways we are blessed right now and are so grateful to get to know new people who want to help.

This is what I must remember: Everything I desire is always available to me. Everything happens for me, not to me. There is always a way through. When I stop forcing and am open to receiving support, I make space for miracles to appear.

My prayer for our community today:

> Help us to see the bounty of gifts we've been given, rather than the things that have been taken away.

# Day 15 of the Apocalypse
## Ground Zero, Gerton, NC, Pop. 301

Our dachshund Winston is not a morning dog. Today, after two weeks of getting up early every day, he decides he is done with our new lifestyle.

When I open the dog crate, at the reasonable hour of 8:00 a.m., he hides. Our other dachshund, Leroy, of course leaps into action. Leroy is food motivated. Winston is self-care motivated.

After turning the generator on, feeding Leroy, and making my breakfast, I eventually go back into our bedroom to discover Winston napping under the covers on my side of the bed, soaking up the warmth I had left behind. I let him be.

Winston finally emerges at 11:00 a.m., ready to be cuddled, but not ready for activities like going outside to pee, especially because he does not consider himself to be a dog. Instead, he climbs into my lap, and wraps his neck around my neck, his way of both comforting and suffocating me.

Winston always knows when it's time for us to rest as a family, so Jeff and I take a rest day today. We stay in our pajamas all day!

We really, really need it. This is the first slow day we've had since the rain started on September 25th.

I clean up around the house, organizing supplies we've been bringing up the mountain. I also go through every item in both of our refrigerators and freezers, purging what has gone bad over the past two weeks and taking an inventory of what food is still good. The watermelon and yogurt didn't make it. The cheese and apples did.

Jeff continues his online efforts to solicit donations (cash, Starlink systems, and small generators). He begins his mornings crouched next to our kitchen island. He's charging his phone while responding to messages, what he does for the first hour of every day.

Jeff gets hundreds of comments and DM messages in response to his daily posts in the "We are Gerton, NC" Facebook group. Some people ask him to check on their home: "Is it still there?" "Is there any visible damage?" They tell Jeff where their house keys are hidden and ask him to go inside to assess water and other damage.

Others ask Jeff to check on the status of particular people: "Have you seen Jim? Is he still alive?" These questions are still posted daily, even though the hurricane happened two weeks ago.

People message Jeff asking what types of supplies they can bring to Gerton and surrounding communities. They want to know where and how to volunteer. Jeff now spends upwards of sixteen hours a day coordinating supplies and responding to messages. He, like many men, is very mission oriented. This is a necessary and very important role. I am so grateful that he stepped up and is doing what he needs to do to help our community.

This morning, Jeff is also fashionably wrapped in a red, doggie blanket, attempting to keep warm, because we don't turn on the heat when the generator is running. Running our HVAC system uses a *lot* of propane, so we're saving that for when we really need it.

Jeff and I spend a couple of hours checking on all of our immediate neighbors' homes (we have keys to everyone's house). We switch off everyone's main power breaker so there will be no power surge when electricity eventually gets restored.

Just a normal day in our apocalyptic neighborhood.

Other news: The first Duke Energy lineworkers arrived in Gerton two days ago. Their first job is to repair power on the main road, so that the fire station has power.

The fire station staff also discovered that their septic system has backed up (probably because so many community members have been relying on their bathrooms). On top of that, their generator has also failed. In addition to everything else they are dealing with, they now need to get both major systems fixed. I imagine their trucks are also getting damaged in the midst of all of this, so there is another unexpected, added cost for them.

The good news is that portable toilets and showers also arrived two days ago, right on time. These will be so helpful to our community members without generators or water, who are able to get to the fire station.

Through all of this, Fire Chief Jay is showing up every single day. He is a kind, direct man. He doesn't view other people as wrong for their opinions and ideas and doesn't appear to take on the brunt of other people's frustrations. Jay is dealing with hundreds of people coming at him every single day. They are asking questions, wanting to help, voicing concerns, and bringing him problems. His wife, Carolyn, remains steadfast beside him, helping to field communications and keep information organized in the control room.

At the end of each community meeting, Jay still closes with a prayer, thanking God for providing for and blessing us.

# Day 16 of the Apocalypse
## Ground Zero, Gerton, NC, Pop. 301

Will and his crew of linemen from Kentucky, with their beautiful, white, electric company trucks, line up along our road. They have accents so thick that, even with my twelve years of living in Appalachia, I can't decipher their words.

The linemen apologize for taking so long to restore our power. I counter with my shock that they have made it to our road already. We thought it would be months before we saw them.

They have a truck that is stuck. Jeff and I are trying to get down our road in our UTV. (Yay! It was delivered to Gerton within forty-eight hours of purchase!) Jeff is driving the UTV, so I get out to see what's going on. The linemen are trying to back the truck up a steep slope in order to install an electric pole about forty feet from the road, but the road is muddy and the truck tires keep slipping.

There are a bunch of guys just standing around, watching another guy unsuccessfully back the truck up, over and over again. I can immediately tell why the truck isn't able to back up. It's because there is a ditch between the road and the slope that needs to be packed with something the truck can drive over to get traction.

So now I'm a road engineer. Add that to my apocalypse resume. I jump into action and direct the men to haul tree trunks lying fallen by the side of the road and stack them up in the ditch. They do, and a few minutes later the truck backs successfully over the trunks and up the slope to the installation site.

I meet John and his crew of skilled sawyers from Shelby, NC, who brilliantly brought their own UTVs with them, making them mobile enough to be able to get up the mountain to our neighborhood.

I climb into one of the UTVs with them, cramming myself in the back seat between Frankie and Billy, who jokes that he hopes I am not wearing perfume, because his wife would smell it on him later. I lead their UTV brigade up our roads, showing them the devastation and sharing stories of what our neighbors have been through.

I sweet talk my way into moving a dozen repair trucks out of the way to get these guys up to the top of our road so they can clear the trees from our neighbors' driveways. They are able to clear the trees completely from Don and Laura's property, which is a big win for Don and Laura.

Their home burned to the ground eleven months ago, right before Christmas, in an accidental fire. Erik and I were both there, he as the first firefighter on scene and me because I heard his fire truck and rushed to see what was happening. Don and Laura were at their home in Charlotte, and I wanted to ensure they were notified as soon as possible. Erik and I watched the roof collapse. By the time we got to the house, the second-floor bathtub was sitting on the front porch.

I had walked by their property just an hour earlier, on my daily route with our dogs, and I didn't even smell smoke. Their house sits down in a holler, away from the road, and is blocked by trees, so unless I made a point of going down their driveway, I wouldn't have seen much. But I should have been able to smell smoke by then.

It was a horrifying experience, with firefighters from four stations in our neighborhood working all night, trying to ensure the fire didn't spread. We had just had a two-week long forest fire on the other side of our mountain a month prior that destroyed several homes.

Don and Laura have been trying to rebuild their home ever since the fire, but with four giant trees lying in a pile across their driveway, there was no way their construction crew could return to work.

Later in the day, I find Sam, a gentle, white-haired man with a youthful face and big glasses, who works at Whole Foods. He is inside our fire station shopping in the Walmart of our thousands of donated supplies. He pulls me aside to confide that if I need a peaceful place to shop, his particular Whole Foods is calm and welcoming. Sam gets it. We've gone to town for groceries twice, and both times the noise and bustle were overwhelming.

Toward the end of the day, Stevie emerges in a haze of cigarette smoke, with a salt and pepper ponytail and deep creases in his suntanned face, making him look at least ten years older than he actually is. He brought a crew, also out of Shelby, NC, along with two giant generators to donate. Stevie needs help finding families to donate the generators to and a place to camp for the night near the fire station.

Dorrien, who has done disaster relief for years, is part of the AVL F.A.S.T. group that Jeff has been working with. Right before we head back up the mountain, he shows up with multiple donated specialty items that Jeff has solicited for our community.

He needs a UTV ride over the mountain to Middle Fork, an area of our fire district that still has eighty people trapped. Dorrien brings a Starlink system with him for that community and also wants to scope out a location there for a helicopter to drop a 500-pound propane tank for the entire community to have access to.

Kyle pulls up in small, black pickup truck behind us as Jeff and I are trying to get back up our mountain in our own UTV. We are waiting for an hour behind electrical trucks for the lineworkers to do what they need to do. Their trucks are blocking a big section of our private road.

Kyle is a small, muscly man with dark-red, tight curls and a large heart-shaped tattoo on his left bicep. He lives down the mountain next to the creek. The flooding destroyed his shed full of most of his equipment for cutting trees. He sells firewood to make a living and was heading up our road to a friend's house to help him clear trees.

Each hour of today feels like a week. There is too much going on now.

# Day 17 of the Apocalypse
## Ground Zero, Gerton, NC, Pop. 301

Today we got power.

Up until today, we spent seventeen days managing our propane consumption and running our whole house generator for only one or two hours each morning and two or three hours in the evening.

We timed everything from showers to cooking, to pooping, to laundry, and to communication with the outside world to fit within those five precious hours.

It was hard to constantly track, organize, and keep our home operational. There wasn't the luxury of just coming home and resting. Even late at night, sitting in the dark, there was always more to be done.

Seventeen days with a total of five minutes of phone calls with the outside world for me because service is still so spotty on my phone.

It was hard to not be able to talk to the people closest to me. But part of me also didn't want to speak with them. I didn't want to hear their concern and their worry about me. There has been no time or space for worry. I can't make room for that right now, and I sure can't explain what I've—what we all have—been through.

Seventeen days of getting to know so many more of my neighbors. Sitting with them on their porches, at the fire station, perched on fallen trees, and talking, listening to their hurricane stories, and learning what happened to their homes and their hearts when Helene hit.

I have also been hearing about all of the old trauma that has been stirred up as a result of this devastation: of women being raped or held hostage and how this disaster has retraumatized them.

I've heard the stories of people having nightmares of being trapped or drowning in water or mud.

I am witnessing loved ones lost. Houses, cars, and animals, gone.

Seventeen days of being so tired that even a good night's sleep isn't enough for me to feel rested.

Yesterday, when we had power and our Starlink signal connected, I needed to look something up online. I went to type in a URL address and literally typed in "internet.com."

So there's that. My brain isn't fully functioning yet.

Seventeen days and probably 300 hours of Jeff coordinating supplies and running his Facebook group. As I type this, he's working on getting a handful of tiny homes to Gerton for our neighbors to live in who lost their homes.

Seventeen days of helicopters flying low over our house twenty-four hours a day. I don't even look anymore. I know what flies over by the sound.

Seventeen days, and I still don't really know how to talk about what happened to us, other than to say it feels like what I imagine a war zone would be like.

I am still so tired. We are all so tired. It is weirdly comforting to know that all pretense is gone. We are casualties in, and comrades of, our common ground, which is exhaustion.

It is exhausting to spend all day getting basic needs met.

It is exhausting to never know what each day will bring.

## The Deep End of Hope in the Wake of Hurricane Helene

It is exhausting to try to explain to anyone who is not living in devastation the toll it takes.

It feels like an aching tiredness, like my body is twice as heavy as it normally is, and each movement takes concentrated effort. I don't understand why my brain won't comprehend or compute, or why my limbs are so uncooperative. Even falling asleep takes work. We are going through the motions of our lives, like zombies.

But we're continuing to do what needs to be done, just like everyone else around us. That is the way, here in Appalachia. It doesn't matter how tired anyone is, how much they have lost or whether they believe in the same things, politically, religiously, or otherwise. Everyone just keeps showing up to do what needs to be done. There's no complaining. We all just thank God for the blessing that is today, and we move on.

Today we'll go down to the fire station. I'll minister to people. Jeff will work on communication and supply coordination. We'll drive into town to grab some groceries for Kate, Erik, Jeff, and I to eat for dinner. I'll have to remind Jeff not to buy bags of ice, because we don't need to use our coolers anymore to keep meat and milk cold.

We'll come home after a long day, and Jeff will have to remind me to turn on lights because I keep operating in the dark.

I have made the darkness my friend. It is safe to me now, even though it exhausts me.

We will have dinner with Erik and Kate, and we'll drink too much. We'll go to bed too late and get up too early, because that's just what our bodies do now.

We will continue to do our part to recover ourselves and our community.

# Day 18 of the Apocalypse
## Ground Zero, Gerton, NC, Pop. 301

Last night, I dreamt that tall trees with no branches kept falling on our roof.

Eventually I realized that the trees were instead power poles. Helicopters were carrying them over our house and dropping them onto our roof.

In my dream, there were a few trees that remained standing in our yard. They each had huge gashes in them, where water had stolen their wood. The gashes were so deep it seemed like the trees would topple over should the wind pick up.

Then the scene shifted, and Jeff and I were trying to escape off of our mountain, but all of the roads had turned into rivers. The water was muddy, dark, and deep. We were wading through the darkness, chest deep. Breathless. We were trying to keep ahead of the momentum of the water. Pushing through it was exhausting.

By the time we reached town, we were soaked. We tried to check into a hotel to get warm and dry our clothes, but we had no money. The woman at reception said she would take just my credit card number instead of a physical card, but I couldn't remember how to operate my phone to look up the number. I knew my brain had done this process hundreds of times, but I couldn't retrieve the information.

These are the types of dreams I still have every night, nearly a month after the hurricane. Trees. Water. Can't escape. No access to resources. Can't think. Everything feels overwhelming.

I am not alone in this. Many people I speak to in our community continue to have nightmares or still aren't sleeping through the night. Nightmares can be a way for the brain to try and make sense of traumatic memories in order to integrate the experience. It is safer to process the trauma in the recesses of our minds, in the middle of the night. During the day, we still have to find ways to move through the devastation in real time.

Maybe this is complex trauma, or PTSD (post-traumatic stress disorder). I don't know. It doesn't matter. I know that my psyche is doing the best it can at this particular time to process what has happened. I am allowing my body and mind the grace to do what they need to do, to move through this. I am not pushing myself to respond any differently.

Traumatic situations affect each of us differently. There is no right way to process them.

In Erwin, TN, about fifty miles north of here, eleven people were swept away by the flood. They were unable to escape rising waters around a plastics factory where they worked. Only five people were rescued. The rest died. Surviving workers said they were not allowed to leave until water had already flooded the plant's parking lot and the power went out.

*Do people really have to wait for someone to tell them to go, when the river is rising?* Yes. When there is too much trauma in their genetics and history, people wait to be told. We all respond differently.

I am writing my way through the apocalypse. This is my biggest coping mechanism for trauma. If I can make sense of what happened through words, then maybe, eventually, my heart and body will be able to heal.

Maybe eventually I will dream of something else.

I know my body is still having a trauma response. I'm sleeping ten hours a night, plus taking a nap every afternoon, and I'm still exhausted.

Maybe eventually I will have slept enough.

There is no right way to dream. No right way to rest. No right way to move through this.

There is only what our bodies and minds are doing and our willingness to submit to what is needed in each moment.

This is how maybe, eventually, we will heal.

# Day 19 of the Apocalypse
## Ground Zero, Gerton, NC, Pop. 301

Over the past two weeks, no one from the Red Cross has shown up in Gerton to offer support. People dressed as Red Cross workers allegedly showed up to loot people's homes.

No one employed by FEMA or any other government entity has shown up.

North Carolina DOT has sent some contractors to assist with road reconstruction, thanks to intervention by State Senator Tim Moffitt (R-NC), who lives on top of our mountain.

No one from FEMA has come to Gerton to assist people in applying for disaster relief. We still have no power/internet/cell phone service in almost all areas of our fire district.

There are other FEMA sites throughout Western North Carolina in larger communities like Asheville, Black Mountain, Hendersonville, Swannanoa, and Weaverville. FEMA employees there are helping people to apply for disaster relief (which right now is only an immediate $750 to cover the cost of lost food). They are also answering questions about emergency assistance options.

So FEMA is around, but not in Hickory Nut Gorge, one of the hardest hit areas where many people do not have a way to enroll for assistance either via phone or internet.

This reinforces the belief that people who live in the most rural parts of Appalachia have always had—that the real Appalachian people never get the support they most need from the government. All of these big disaster organizations who are supposed to be leading the efforts of our recovery, are nowhere to be found.

Additionally, outside of myself and three other Gerton community members (including the pastor of our Baptist church), there are no professionals assisting us with mental, emotional, or spiritual care.

It took four days for anyone from the outside world to even get to us.

The military has shown up for us, over and over again, landing giant Chinooks (helicopters with two propellers) filled with pallets of supplies, including, of course, hundreds of cases of bottled water. Black Hawk helicopters were the first on the scene, assessing damage to our Gorge from above. The National Guard were the ones evacuating people from our mountain by helicopter. The 101st Airborne Division also showed up a few days ago, to help clear roads.

The North Carolina DOT and Kentucky DOT have worked diligently on our roads. Duke Energy lineworkers are here every day working on our power.

Charleston Police Department, North Carolina State Patrol, and others have been handling our checkpoint occasionally since last week, freeing community members and our firefighters to attend to other pressing needs.

Hundreds of volunteers, either related to/connected to the Gerton community or simply showing up on their own, have brought in supplies and willing hands.

Many church groups have volunteered, especially Chestnut Ridge Baptist of Kings Mountain, NC and Grace Baptist Church, out of Gastonia, NC. They work together at a food truck at our fire station and are delivering 400 hot meals a day to community members and first responders. Jeff loves everything about this food truck, as his appetite has not been affected by the apocalypse.

Our Volunteer Fire Department has been working nonstop since Day 1 to ensure that every community member is accounted for, cared for, and able to get the support they need.

We are Gerton strong. We are each doing our part to help our community recover and will continue to do so when outside support dries up.

This is how we handle things in a small community in Appalachia. We show up and help one another. We don't expect anyone else to help us.

It's discouraging when lack of support from disaster relief organizations and our government is confirmed.

Everything that has happened in our community over the past two weeks has happened because of people choosing to come together. I've been paying close attention to who those people are.

Most of them I would not agree with, politically. I've been learning very quickly that in order to survive this apocalypse, and truly be a part of this community, I've had to set aside political division. This is what has allowed me to trust people who are different from me. This is what enables me to be open to them and receive all the gifts they have to offer. This is the greatest form of Love, to recognize that we are all 360-degree people. There are a myriad of ways to understand and appreciate other people.

There are a lot of mountains I've been climbing down since the storm. One I'd already started climbing down, after moving to rural Appalachia twelve years ago, was the one where my political beliefs are right, and others' political beliefs are wrong, because when shit gets real, it doesn't matter.

What matters is who actually shows up and does the hard things.

Tonight, there was a blessing in the sky over our community. The aurora borealis, also known as the northern lights, appeared in gorgeous pink and purple tones. The sun collided with the Earth's magnetic field and created awestriking beauty shining down on us, reminding us that renewal and transformation are possible.

## Day 20 of the Apocalypse
### Ground Zero, Gerton, NC, Pop. 301

Our next-door neighbor Kate is a botanist and sawyer. The woman knows how to wield a chainsaw in remarkable ways. She has been leading saw crews in our community since Day 2. A few days ago, she led a crew in clearing dozens of trees off the road that goes to our friends Stan and Dave's house.

This is one of the roads we were most concerned about, as it was taking Stan and Dave two hours to walk to the fire station, normally a twenty-minute trip.

A beloved, sixty-nine-year-old member of our community was part of Kate's crew. She showed us a video of him scaling one of the fallen giant poplars to cut it. He cut steps in the poplar trunk in order to climb it, and an excavator held the tree in place to relieve pressure and assist with safety for this very technical cut.

There are many more trees like this in our community that still need to be cut down.

Kate and Erik also led a mission with thirty-six members of the 101st Airborne Division yesterday to our friend Myrtle's neighborhood. The men were hyped up and excited to get to work.

Kate and Erik trained the men to start and operate a chainsaw. It has become normal for Kate to lead saw crews with half skilled and half unskilled workers. Kate felt such an overabundance of help with the number of men present, that it was hard to assign tasks. There were only three saws, and she and Erik had two of them. The men tried to compensate by using axes to hack at trees in the road. Because of the mudslide conditions, there was a fine rock mixture on the trunks of the trees, and the chainsaws were dulling immediately. In just one day, members of the 101st sharpened each chainsaw a dozen times.

Kate noticed these guys were incredibly good at lifting heavy objects and moving them, which was perfect for the task at hand: moving rocks and trees off a road so it could be rebuilt.

Then they reached Myrtle's house and discovered a massive landslide right next to her house, covering her driveway and car.

During the storm, Myrtle had hunkered down with her cat in her bathroom, the only room without windows. That Friday morning around 9:30 a.m., shortly before the rain let up, she felt what seemed like an earthquake.

She went to the window, and saw a landslide down her driveway, with boulders bigger than her car cartwheeling by, along with several large trees. The landslide knocked her propane tank a quarter mile away, along with her barn.

Myrtle knew she had to leave her house immediately, in case another mudslide happened. She had prepacked a backpack with clothes and cat food. She went outside to determine a route to take off her property but realized there was no way she could take her cat with her.

Mud came all the way up her porch, so she knew she couldn't walk down the driveway. Myrtle attempted to walk out behind her house, which is up against a steep slope, with a road at the top of the slope. She bushwhacked her way up the slope, only to discover that the mudslide was also blocking that entire road too.

There were giant trees and power lines down everywhere. The road in front of her house had become a river with waterfalls in it. It took her one and a half hours to get to her next-door neighbor's house, which is normally a five-minute walk. Myrtle was in shock, as were her neighbors. No one had any idea what to do.

Jenn, the firefighter who helped the people at Trillium Court, checked on them that afternoon. Myrtle chose not to return to her house that night because she didn't know if it was safe from future mudslides.

On Day 2, she did make her way back, fed the cat, and packed up a cooler and big bag of supplies to take to the neighbor's house, where she decided to stay for the time being. Their home was unscathed. Without propane, Myrtle had no generator power, water, heat, or ability to cook.

Myrtle began hearing on the radio that there was no water or power in Asheville. Myrtle thought staying in her neighborhood was best, where supply drops were being made and she had access to showers at yet another neighbor's house. If she were to evacuate, she had no idea where she would go, or what to do with her cat. Without cell service, she couldn't contact anyone. Myrtle felt like she would be safer staying.

Finally, on Day 5, she and another neighbor hiked up to the top of their mountain, Burntshirt Mountain, which has a vineyard at the top. They ate their weight in grapes and attempted to use their cell phones. Myrtle had one bar of service and retrieved a message from friends in nearby Etowah. They offered to pick her up from any helicopter landing zone and gave her use of their Airbnb and extra car to use indefinitely.

Myrtle bawled her eyes out, grateful that she had a way out for herself and her cat. She knew she needed to get off the mountain and start working again to pay for her mortgage and the extensive damage. All roads below here were destroyed. Her home was uninhabitable, especially as the weather got colder.

Myrtle also didn't want to be a strain on the recovery efforts. She knew that some people had refused to evacuate and were drawing heavily on resources and manpower. She considered "the path of least resistance for everyone" and decided to evacuate.

When she went to the helicopter landing zone the next morning, the Black Hawk was full but offered to come back two hours later to pick up Myrtle and her cat. Myrtle raced back to her house, cleaning out her fridge as much as possible, drugging her cat for comfort, and leaving out food, camping, and medical supplies for her neighbors. She left her front door open, so anyone could help themselves.

Myrtle had been in a helicopter before, and was fine, but the cat wasn't having it. He screamed the entire time, fighting his way around the carrier that was clipped in next to her. She is now resting a lot, enjoying spending time with friends, and slowly returning to work. Myrtle is trying to be patient with herself as her concentration is diminished; she can't get her brain to work how it used to, and she struggles with constantly hearing about other people's trauma when they come into her doctor's office.

When Kate and the 101st arrived at Myrtle's house a few weeks later, they dug out her car from the mudslide. People like Myrtle, who have evacuated, are relying heavily on those of us on the ground here to help them address the hundreds of thousands of dollars of destruction that they are faced with, which insurance or FEMA may not pay for. Kate's mission today was to help alleviate Myrtle's burden, moving forward.

There was a lot of mud underneath Myrtle's car, so the Airborne men offered to simply lift it up and move it. Kate thought that was funny but not necessary. They did get her car out. Kate also went into Myrtle's house to grab her a bunch of extra winter clothes, as Myrtle doesn't plan on returning to her house until the spring.

It is fantastic, and poignant, to imagine Kate, who is a stunning, highly educated woman, commanding the entire thirty-six-member 101st Airborne Division. We are all becoming people we've never been before. This is Transformational Love.

## Day 21 of the Apocalypse
## Ground Zero, Gerton, NC, Pop. 301

I found out this week that my forty-eight-year-old brother Bryce died by suicide.

Bryce was a gentle soul. He struggled with drug and alcohol addiction, including several overdoses, for nearly four decades. My prayers are with his three children, who lost their father way too early. I understand their pain. Our father also died when he was forty-eight.

May Bryce rest in the peace he's been searching for his entire life.

Less than three months ago, our forty-year-old brother Alex died by suicide.

Three years ago this week, our thirty-five-year-old brother Edward died by suicide.

Three weeks ago today, Hurricane Helene destroyed our mountain community, and hundreds of lives were lost.

I am surrounded by death.

I am consumed by devastation.

I got the call about Bryce from my mother's best friend, Mary Jane, a woman I haven't spoken to in thirty years. My mother and I have had almost no contact for fifteen years, because it's too easy for me to get swept back into the drama of her mental illness. My best, most effecttive, adult coping mechanism is to distance myself from my family.

Without conscious thought, I broke into a guttural, animal, fall-to-my-knees, hand-to-God cry for help. I was sitting on the front stoop of my mother-in-law Linda's house in Fairview.

We had just been in her backyard, assessing the work that her tree company had completed, clearing four dozen fallen trees from her house and yard in record time. Only four of the trees had fallen on her house. Insurance covered lifting those four trees off the house, but not hauling them away or grinding their stumps. To date, they have not agreed to repair the damage to her roof.

Linda was in the process of having the tree stumps ground, and her entire backyard regraded and seeded, so that grass would grow again. Her next step was to plant new trees, to replace a few of the old ones. All in all, this was a $100,000 out-of-pocket expense for her. She is eighty-four years old. Like almost everyone else we know in this area, this is an expenditure she cannot afford, especially on a fixed income. She joked with me that she'll just have to die a little sooner, in order to get by.

Linda's not alone in this. We have friends who are selling their houses, because they cannot afford the repairs, or cannot fathom them, or both.

I was trying to connect Linda's tree company with our nearby neighbors, Paul and Susan, who have a fifty-foot-tall chestnut tree precariously tipping next to their home, overshadowing their cabin. That tree removal requires a crane and technical skill. This company would be the perfect fit for their needs.

Then I checked my phone, and Mary Jane had left me a message. *Unusual.* I thought for a moment my mother had died, but instead, Bryce had. After decades of near-death experiences, he was finally gone.

Mary Jane was only able to speak with me for a few minutes, as she was at a doctor's appointment. I learned that Bryce had overdosed.

# The Deep End of Hope in the Wake of Hurricane Helene

Our mother hadn't heard from Bryce for a few days, so she requested a welfare check by law enforcement. The people doing the welfare check found Bryce dead in his apartment.

Instead of driving the three miles between her apartment and his, to check on Bryce herself, our mother had a stranger check on him. She must have known something bad had happened; she's always been intuitive like that.

Bryce had been clean for twenty months leading up to his death, one of his longer stretches of sobriety.

Three months ago, I was the one who called our mother, when I was the first notified about Alex's death. A detective in the town where Alex was living had called to tell me Alex had hanged himself. He told me he found my name and number in a database that police have access to for tracing family relations. That slightly creeps me out. This was exactly how I was notified about our father's death twenty-six years ago. I was listed as next of kin, instead of our mother.

I do not want to be in this database.

Alex's dying was the second time I had to tell our mother that one of our family members died. The first time was with our father. The sheriff of the small town where Dad lived had also tracked me down. He had been dead in his apartment for three days before he was found.

With Alex, I put on my trauma chaplain hat and decided to break the news to our mother as if I was a caring first responder, attending to a distraught family member. That helped.

But when Bryce died, our mother did not have the courage to call me and tell me herself. She hid behind a friend. If she had been the one to call me, she might have had to acknowledge that our childhood had something to do with Bryce's death. And Alex's. And our younger brother Edward's death three years ago.

I am a petulant child again, wanting my mother to be someone she is incapable of being.

After I hung up the phone with Mary Jane, I went inside Linda's house, searching for Jeff, to tell him the news. I encountered my brother-in-law Greg first. He is a math professor at a university here in Asheville, and prides himself on being able to create logical solutions to any problem. I have always experienced him as kind and considerate, but not outwardly emotional.

Greg had heard me wailing and asked me what was wrong. "My brother fucking killed himself" was my instant reply, before my entire body started heaving in sobs. I was so mad at Bryce for choosing to die two weeks after the hell of Helene. I was still overwhelmed with figuring out how to live each day. *How dare he, once again, make this about him?* So much of my life has been about Bryce's addiction.

Remarkably, Greg grabbed onto me tight, until eventually Jeff arrived and took over. Jeff and I just looked at each other, knowing that there were no words of consolation available for this lineage of suicide in my family.

Later Jeff told me that he heard my wailing from the garage. He thought it was the sound of a wild animal, trapped. Then he thought it must be his mother, learning of the death of a close relative. It never occurred to him that I would lose yet another brother to suicide, especially at this particular time.

He is right. It is inexplicable.

As I write this, sitting outside on a beautiful blue-sky day, four crows, symbols of death, instantly converge in the tree above me.

For me, they represent my three brothers and our father who died by suicide twenty-six years ago. I choose to believe this means that my brothers and father have found each other in the afterlife.

I am safe.

I am fed.

I am warm.

## The Deep End of Hope in the Wake of Hurricane Helene

I am embraced by loving arms.

I am held by a power greater than myself.

I am watched over.

I am blessed.

# Day 22 of the Apocalypse
## Ground Zero, Gerton, NC, Pop. 301

Jeff and I attended church together this week, a first for our marriage. I'm a Quaker minister and shamanic practitioner; he is a non-practicing Catholic. We went to a Baptist service at the only church in our small community.

The pews were filled with church members as well as other community members. This was fun to see. Gerton is surprisingly diverse. On the surface we don't look it, as our community is predominately white, which is typical in rural Appalachia.

We have liberals, conservatives, and libertarians here. There is a thriving gay community, several artists, as well as blue collar, white collar, and no collar workers. We run the gamut from atheism to old school Baptist, with everything from a tarot reader and a Sufi, and of course me, a Quaker, thrown into the mix. There is incredible economic diversity, ranging from people living in trailers off the grid because that is all they can afford, to people living in six-million-dollar homes.

In the pews were also several members of the Disaster Relief EMS, as well as North Carolina Highway Patrol, one of whom even served as pianist during the service.

The pianist, a gentle, black man, joyous to find himself in church among strangers, led us in a beautiful gospel hymn about giving yourself away (in service to others). Jeff teared up as he sang along.

Pastor Donnie, a small, seventy-nine-year-old, white man, born and raised in Gerton, with a big smile and a large cross on his tie, also spoke about using the talent that God gave us, in service to others.

Our Fire Chief, Jay, led us in "Amazing Grace." It felt good to be with many of our neighbors in the sanctuary.

There was some commentary on evolution offered during the service that didn't quite resonate with me. Something about how "if we came from monkeys, how could monkeys still exist?" (That question actually stuck with me for a hot minute.) Or "we don't come from amoebas." I think the pastor actually was stating that he doesn't believe we were originally single-cell organisms.

During the sermon, there was judgment against people in our community who did not attend church that day. The church service apparently had been quite crowded the week before, in what Pastor Donnie called a 9/11 response. Something terrible happens, and all of a sudden even atheists and non-Baptists are finding God. But then the next week we're back to things as usual, with most of the community not in attendance.

I understand that. When something happens that is unimaginable, we cannot help but to search for answers, and often, that means looking for a higher power to help make sense out of it all. I had lots of people call on me when I worked as a trauma chaplain who might not otherwise have asked for support. When we are in crisis, we want to know there is someone greater than us looking out for us. We want to feel comforted and held by something other than humanity, which can be weak and frail.

I don't have to agree with the pastor in order to feel comforted or closer to God or my community because I know the sacred is available to me regardless of where I am sitting on Sunday morning.

## The Deep End of Hope in the Wake of Hurricane Helene

Two days ago, my neighbor Julia, a Sufi minister, invited me into her home for an energy healing. I needed it. My nervous system was already depleted from the apocalypse, and my body responded to my brother's suicide with another raging migraine.

I spent most of the day prior lying on the floor in front of our wood stove, soaking up the warmth and icing my head for relief. Our dogs wrapped their long dachshund bodies around me, offering protection, matching my pain with their peace.

I lay on Julia's massage table in her beautiful upstairs office. She put a weighted blanket on me, and spent time blessing me, and praying for me and my brother, in both English and Arabic.

As Julia laid hands on me, I felt the room fill with angels and guides. I felt my body being wrapped and carried in a long shallow boat, along the Euphrates River.

Later, I learned the Euphrates symbolizes God's power over the natural world. Biblically, God is in all things, including hurricanes and devastation. In the Hebrew Bible, the Euphrates is also seen as a geographic marker that delineates belonging and exclusion.

Hurricane Helene is also a symbolic delineation. In response to her, we chose belonging over exclusion.

Julia kept asking for mercy to be bestowed upon me. *Rachman*, the essence of the divine quality of mercy, was the word/sound she repeated while laying her hands on my feet, my heart, and the top of my head.

*Rachman* is the most gracious and most merciful. The one who brings blessings and compassion and that which connects us with the truth of who we are.

> May the most merciful have mercy upon you.
>
> May God bless you and keep you.
>
> May the Light in you find the Light in others.

Lord and Father, almighty and eternal God, by your blessing you give us strength and support in our frailty.

Earth Mother, surround us with your loving arms. Shelter us from what we cannot bear alone. Help us to be a contribution to others.

It's easy for religious differences to create division, especially during times of devastation. The courageous path is to keep searching for unity.

All prayers belong now.

All religions offer peace now.

All beliefs that bring comfort are welcome now.

This is the theology of grace.

Hurricane Helene didn't happen to us. She happened for us.

She showed us what matters: community, receiving support, being blessed, and blessing others.

## Reflections on Trauma in the Recovery Phase

In the recovery phase, we begin to consider the bounty of the gifts we have been given, rather than the things that have been taken away. We express gratitude for what we have, giving thanks that we are still alive.

There is also a recognition that we are all becoming people we've never been before.

For some of us, that looks like learning to live differently, temporarily relocating, living in tents or campers or living with friends or extended family members. All of us who remain are learning how to live in the devastation, with damage to homes or properties or with no potable water or power.

Moving out of shock and disbelief, PTSD (post-traumatic stress disorder) symptoms begin to kick in. People are irritable, having mood swings, anxiety, or depression. I can recall multiple times speaking alongside the fire chief at the community meeting about how people were acting up, and how we needed as a community to keep the focus on being loving towards one another.

Lots of people, including myself, were having flashbacks or nightmares, like the memories of that morning, huddled in bed with Jeff, hearing, but not yet knowing the extent of the devastation, or the moment Erik told us about the destruction below us, or neighbors telling their stories of flooding and barely making it out alive.

It took three weeks for me to even be able to sleep through the night, and when I did start sleeping, I couldn't get enough of it. No amount of sleep was sufficient to heal my exhaustion.

I was never able to eat real food when I was down at the fire station or attending to people. It's like my body just shut that part of me down because it was using all its resources to keep me standing.

My migraines, which I had finally gotten a handle on after nearly forty years of suffering with them weekly, came back with a vengeance, often in two- or three-day stints. Kate started feeling her heart racing on a regular basis. Others spoke to me about their panic attacks or inability to do things.

Everyone around us, including Jeff and me, were having a hard time making decisions. We also forgot how to do the most basic of things, like how I couldn't recall how to use the internet, after three weeks of not having access to it.

It's hard to predict when PTSD will set in with survivors of a traumatic natural disaster or in my case with a natural disaster and a death in my family. Some people at first seemed perfectly (or even abnormally) fine, only to have symptoms show up later with a vengeance. Others started showing symptoms immediately. There is no right time for symptoms to show up. There's no scorecard.

The general litmus test for mental health is whether symptoms manifest or continue beyond the first month following a disaster.

People also do not need to have experienced the disaster firsthand to be psychologically affected. I saw this all over social media in the wake of Helene. People subjected to countless hours of television coverage and social media posts, coupled with an inability to get information about their own family or the situation, experienced panic and overwhelm. A disaster has an emotional impact on people regardless of whether they were in the disaster when it happened.

The real work of recovery and healing is a willingness to transform in the wake of disaster. This is the journey of Transformational Love, where remembrance, mourning, and acceptance mold each of us into who we are becoming.

During recovery, we enter the journey of Transformational Love. This is the real work of healing, being willing to transform, rather than trying to return to what and who we were before Helene.

During this period of recovery, I found offering up this prayer to be helpful:

> You are a victory.
>
> The very act of getting up, yet again, and choosing to face the day, is victorious.
>
> The future is uncontrollable. All you have is this moment.
>
> And in this moment, you are standing, and you are doing what needs to be done, right now.
>
> That is the act of recovery and healing.
>
> You are transforming through the simple choice to show up and keep going.
>
> It is your birthright to become a person who can recover, who can heal.
>
> In this journey you are divinely held and divinely protected.
>
> Let this truth seep into you and give you comfort.

# PART 3
# RECONSTRUCTION

## Day 23 of the Apocalypse
### Ground Zero, Gerton, NC, Pop. 301

The week of the hurricane I was due for a haircut.

I attempted to call my salon on Jeff's working cell phone, three days after the hurricane hit, to cancel my appointment. We were still trapped on our mountain and couldn't get into town.

The call wouldn't go through. The error message said the phone line didn't exist anymore. I sat there, with Jeff's phone next to my ear, listening to the *dah-dah-dah* sound of the error message multiple times, because the information I was being provided did not compute. *How could a phone line no longer exist?*

Now I know. I've seen the devastation downtown, especially near rivers. Businesses were washed away or completely flooded—up to the ceiling or higher. There's this video that keeps going around on Facebook of a Walgreens at a major intersection next to the Swannanoa River. All you can see is the green of its roof. Rushing water consumed the rest of the building, the parking lot, and the roads on both sides.

Almost all of the River Arts District was washed away, home to so many of our local artists. Our friends Dave and Mike showed me the pieces of artwork (metal and pottery) they had been able to salvage from their gallery. The pieces are covered in thick, dried mud. They hope to clean them up and resell them as part of a "Helene collection."

Destruction videos are constantly popping up on my social media feed. I limit the time I am scrolling through, not because I don't want to know about all the destruction that occurred, but because it's too much to take in all at once. I have learned that I must pace myself with everything I am exposed to.

I am not alone in this thinking. Many people who I've spoken with have mixed feelings about their cell phones working again. They came to appreciate only having to deal with what was going on in Gerton. To know there are other parts of our area with similar devastation and destruction is daunting.

There are images from social media that still haunt me: A photo of grandparents and their seven-year-old grandson stranded on the roof of their house, just moments before the roof collapsed and all three died. A woman hanging onto a tree for dear life, surrounded by a raging river, just moments before she was consumed by it. A family from Ukraine escaping war, and relocating to North Carolina, only to be swallowed by the river and found, days later, nine miles downstream. Images of family albums and other very personal items being found weeks later, miles from their origination. Rivers filled with dead cattle and horses.

Our friend and Gerton firefighter Jacob lost one of his good friends and mentors, Battalion Chief Tony Garrison. On September 27th, Tony and his nephew Brandon Ruppe attempted to rescue a family after a mudslide in a part of Fairview called Craigtown. The area was named Craigtown because it is almost entirely comprised of members of the Craig family from several generations. In the middle of the rescue, homes were consumed by another mudslide, and a total of eleven lives were lost, Tony, Brandon, and nine members of the Craig family.

Jacob, in the midst of his incredible grief over the loss of his friend, reached out to me today to check on me, as I grieve the loss of my brother. That was a kind and generous act.

## The Deep End of Hope in the Wake of Hurricane Helene

Those moments of kindness are what are getting us through this. We all need respites from the too-much-ness of this reality.

I eventually got an email from my hair salon, saying the salon was completely flooded and was temporarily relocated. The email indicated my stylist was still dealing with the aftereffect of the hurricane. They weren't sure when/if she would be available to cut my hair.

Of course, I prayed for her, hoping that she and her family were safe. That is still the prayer for every person we know here in Western North Carolina.

> May they be safe.
>
> May they be warm.
>
> May they be fed.
>
> May their home be intact.

But the thing you need to understand is that it took me twelve long years of living here to finally find the perfect hair stylist.

It was no small feat on my part a year ago to get on the short list of clients my stylist, Vanessa, would see at the salon. She is in high demand and only works a few weeks each month.

Vanessa gets everything about my hair, and doesn't ask me annoying questions like, "How much should I trim off?" or "Where do you want your hair to be parted?"

No one knows the right answers to these questions. We're all just making wild guesses in an attempt to placate our stylists.

Vanessa never asks me questions. She just does her magic.

It felt too overwhelming to contemplate finding another hair stylist while living in an apocalypse or really at any time in the foreseeable future.

In an attempt to comfort myself and get my hair handled I took sewing scissors and hacked at my bangs.

It did not go well.

So Jeff, bless his heart, tracked down our hair stylist on Instagram, offering her obscene amounts of money to cut our hair. Jeff said we would meet her anywhere she was comfortable, even if that meant getting our hair cut in the parking lot of the Food Lion.

Vanessa invited us over to her house to cut my hair as well as Jeff's. Actually, she gave us the option of meeting her in a busy hair salon, or in her peaceful guest cottage, and we opted for the cottage. Too much noise and normalcy still overwhelms us.

Vanessa's house didn't sustain any damage. In fact, she had a hurricane-resistant metal roof put on only weeks before Helene struck.

It was so completely comforting and life-giving to get my hair cut. Thank you, Vanessa, for your quiet, calm environment, good company, and fantastic haircut. Thank you for giving me a moment of just-enough-ness.

This is the part of this new reality we are in that I deeply appreciate. Most of us are doing what we can to positively impact others, regardless of what's going on for us personally.

## Day 24 of the Apocalypse
## Ground Zero, Gerton, NC, Pop. 301

About a week after the hurricane, I started to get weird Prepper ads showing up in my Facebook feed occasionally. Now they are constant.

Every fourth post is an ad for a portable shower, toilet, or generator. There are ads for water filtration systems, walkie-talkies, emergency radios, life-saving medicines, and backpacks full of food and supplies to last anywhere from a week to a month.

Then there are more morbid ads for gas masks, pepper spray projectile guns, and disaster survival books.

Every four posts I am reminded how unprepared we were for the hurricane.

Every four posts I am given curated images of what it looks like to be prepared.

We were not prepared. Even with everything we know now, we could never be fully prepared for an event such as this, because people cannot equip their hearts for mass destruction and devastation. How does one plan for this level of grief?

As my neighbor Laura said to me last night, grief is the most universal human emotion. The more you grieve, the more you give witness to what you have lost.

Where are the ads for healing your heart?

Where is the guidebook for longing for a community that will never exist again?

What ad will give me the tool to process the fact that recovery of bodies still continues just down the road from us, nearly a month after the hurricane? Those are the ads I want to see.

You cannot equip your heart for mass destruction and devastation.

Here are some things that have helped significantly as we have been navigating this brave new world:

- Right before our power went out, I filled seventeen quart-sized Ziploc bags with water and froze them. I divided those bags of ice between our two freezers. Between the ice bags and running our generator for three to five hours a day, we were able to keep all our frozen food frozen. Nothing spoiled, which is miraculous after seventeen days of no power.

- While we still had power, we also filled our bathtub in case we needed water to flush toilets with. I filled every type of jug we had with filtered water, in case we needed drinking water and couldn't access ours because our well pump is run by electricity. We also have a big stand-alone Berkey water filter that we kept filled.

- We had a good stash of batteries for flashlights, as well as rechargeable flashlights. We had two small, rechargeable lamps that we carried around with us from room to room to light our way. They are nicer than flashlights, because they have bases, and you don't need to hold them to direct the light.

- We learned how to extend the functionality of our generator by turning off the main power from the generator to the house before turning on the generator. That way, when the generator was first turned on, it only had to power itself, not itself plus our entire house. That lessened the wear and tear on our generator, since we were turning it on and off multiple times a day.

- Our hiking packs with water bladder inserts kept us hydrated during the day and allowed us to carry things back up the mountain. Add to that our hiking boots to navigate our now-rugged terrain.

- A chainsaw, to cut up fallen trees. Chainsaw oil and replacement chain. Saw gas.

- The UTV (side-by-side) we bought because hiking down and up the mountain every day (three miles each way) isn't sustainable on top of everything else we are doing. Also, because we need to be able to get supplies to our house and can't always rely on someone else with a UTV being available to cart us and all of our stuff, back up the mountain. We bought one with a four-wheel drive feature, as well as a roof for the driver and passenger and a big bed in the back with enough room for two people to sit in, if needed. The bed can also tilt, which is useful for hauling storm debris around and unloading it easily.

- Our wood stove, in our living room, is powerful enough to heat the front half of our house. We began using it a few days ago when the weather turned cold.

We continue to have dinner every night with Erik and Kate, our next-door neighbors. I set the table with cloth napkins and a candle, even after the power was restored, to welcome us together. It is the main event of our day, where we catch up on activities and news.

We take turns washing dishes, and now that we have power, we usually watch a movie together after dinner. This helps us to create a sense of normalcy.

When the power was out, we cooked all our dinners on our outdoor propane grill, originally by design to conserve generator power inside the house. We also discovered we could readily get twenty-pound containers of propane at the Walmart-of-donated-supplies inside of our fire station, to refuel our grill.

Dinner is always some kind of meat (or veggie burger for Kate, who is a vegan) and vegetables like cabbage or zucchini, which stored well in our sort-of-cold refrigerator. We add potatoes, corn, or microwaved packets of rice or lentils for carbs.

There are other things I wish we would have thought to stock up on before the hurricane like saw gas and oil, generator oil, dog food, electrolytes, protein drinks, fast food (like Tasty Bite's Organic Seasoned Lentil packs that you microwave for ninety seconds), and alcohol.

Just for future reference, in the event of a natural disaster, you're going to want to have the option of a glass of something at the end of an excruciatingly long day. Anytime friends or part-time neighbors came to Gerton to bring supplies, they'd check with us in advance about what "special" supplies we would need. Wine and bourbon made the list a few times.

In retrospect, it would have been super helpful to have a lot more cash on hand. At first, grocery stores weren't even open, but then once they did open, none of them had credit card machines that worked. Early on, our neighbor Walter came up from Charleston with his son Peter to bring us supplies and assess damage to his property. We had mentioned credit card machines were out, so Walter brought $1,000 in cash in case we needed it. Because, you know, banks were closed, internet and power were out, ATMs weren't working, and there was no way for us to get cash ourselves. Cash became king, real fast.

Jeff and I are taking some steps to be more prepared, should we find ourselves in another situation with no power for an extended amount of time or with limited or no cell service. We have become Preppers, by default.

## Day 25 of the Apocalypse
### Ground Zero, Gerton, NC, Pop. 301

We're at a beach outside of Charleston, South Carolina, for a much needed respite.

Forty-five minutes into our drive, there are no signs of devastation. The warm weather and brilliant day allow me to notice, for the first time, that the leaves on the trees have all changed color.

All of my memories from the past three weeks are associated with place, yet it took until today for me to even notice that the brilliance of autumn, here in our mountains, has already fully arrived.

These are some of the places that define my recent memories:

- Huddled under the covers in bed with Jeff and our dogs, during the worst of the hurricane, listening to the trees crack, and having no idea what we would see when the wind and rain stopped.
- First learning about the devastation below us in the Gorge, sitting in the dark on our neighbors' couch, after Erik finally hiked home from down the mountain on Day 1 after the storm ended.
- Learning about first responders who hiked out three miles to stay overnight with people trapped in a house that had collapsed, all of whom were injured.

- Hearing about mudslides that were impassable. Roads littered with fallen trees. Thirty-foot chasms where roads used to exist. Houses and cars that had disappeared.

- Three houses on a hill that all slid simultaneously down the hill, and then further down what used to be the highway, each with families inside.

- The firefighters realizing they had no cell service and no way to contact the outside world, even their county headquarters. The shock of recognizing that no one could contact us or access us, except by air. Noticing that nothing was flying overhead.

- Talking with Fire Chief Jay outside the station early morning on Day 4, learning about my first trauma case: a family who just lost a two-year-old. Watching him tear up, delivering the news.

- Sitting in the middle of the field near our house on Day 3, watching a Black Hawk helicopter fly directly above us; me uncontrollably bursting into tears with the first sign of outside assistance.

- Standing in line with community members at the food truck for free meals, all of us walking around like zombies, unable to have coherent conversations. Focusing on getting our basic needs met, because on most days that is all each of us is capable of doing, even three weeks in.

- Sitting in the parking lot of the fire station with my friend Julia on Day 10, watching a Chinook helicopter circle above us, getting ready to land, to deliver pallets of food and water. Julia, later showing me a photo she took of the woman pilot who flew the helicopter, the most difficult of all to navigate with its two rotors.

- Offering Old Edward a ride to the fire station, as I drove along our broken road in our UTV, to save him from walking another mile to get lunch. His tiny red house, in a holler next to a creek, somehow miraculously surviving the hurricane, although water flowed all around it. Edward is still without water, and hasn't been able to shower in a week, but took time to comfort me when he found out my brother died.

- Standing outside the port-a-potties yesterday, in what used to be the parking lot of our post office, seeing a FEMA worker for the first time twenty-four days after Helene hit.

- Jeff, sitting across from me on our couch, calmly telling me our lives were about to change forever.

Place has defined each of these moments for me. Today I get to notice new things, like the color of the leaves, and in a few hours, ocean waves crashing against the shore.

Today I get to be someone who is not living in devastation. Or at least I thought that was the case. Jeff and I stopped at the grocery store at the beach this evening to pick up a few items, and the woman at the cash register immediately asked us if we were from Western North Carolina. I guess we now look devastated, too. We were too shocked by her observation to ask how she knew.

I can't see myself in perspective. I don't know how I would feel, or what I would look like, if I was outside of Helene. Would I have as much empathy for the Appalachian people as I do right now? Would I be railing at the lack of support for our community being offered by our government and disaster organizations? Would I have already moved on, like the news cycle has?

Would I have a trauma response every time I read a story or see an image of the fallout in the wake of Helene? Possibly. I think it depends on one's previous relationship with hurricanes, and the affected area, and if they knew anyone who lived wherever the devastation was happening.

I'd like to think I'd be a bigger person and still try to be in the trenches of what is happening in our area. But I probably wouldn't. I'd have moved on too, focusing on what's next in my business and in our life. I'd donate money and "hope for the best outcome."

It's easy to focus on something when catastrophe first strikes, and when there are questions you want answered. Are my loved ones alive? Was the damage extensive? How did this happen? Has help arrived? For a few moments, we are all in the experience together. Once those questions are answered, it becomes much easier for the mind to move on.

This is the plight of the Appalachian people. Hundreds of years of not having catastrophes big enough to get media attention or the attention of the rest of the country. Hundreds of years of living in poverty and being ignored by our government.

It is easy to ignore people who do not fight to be seen.

This is how an entire culture developed here in the mountains, of people just doing what needs to get done, without asking for help. When help arrives, they do not trust it. It becomes a threat, rather than an opportunity.

This is how conspiracy theories begin, and burgeoning ones abound.

Earlier this month, a militia group threatened to kill FEMA workers in nearby Chimney Rock, NC, about five miles down the road from us. At the time, search and recovery continued for missing people and dead bodies.

Posts on Facebook and X racked up thousands of views with politically tinged outrage and accusations of secret government meetings and plans to seize the ruined remains of Chimney Rock.

The group claimed that the federal government was taking all of the land and bulldozing the remaining buildings. They stated that property was being confiscated so all of Hickory Nut Gorge could be turned into a lithium mine. They said that dead bodies were piled up in the rubble, the true death toll hidden by callous officials and complicit rescue workers. It was enough to prompt the Rutherford

County government to issue a press release on October 3rd offering a rebuttal:

"NO GOVERNMENT SEIZURE OF CHIMNEY ROCK: There was no 'special meeting' held in Chimney Rock on October 2nd involving discussions of the federal, state, or local governments seizing the town. 'These claims are entirely false,' county officials wrote, explaining that local leaders met with state lawmakers and congressional staff to give an update on relief efforts and advocate for more aid. 'Our focus is solely on recovery, safety, and providing support to those affected by the storm.'"

As of October 1st, Rutherford County had reported three storm-related deaths, and forty-four active missing person investigations.

Being so close to Chimney Rock and closely connected with firefighters and first responders in that area, we absolutely know those claims are false.

But there is a reason claims like these are made and believed—because Appalachian people for hundreds of years have been disenfranchised. They have turned their distaste for government into a belief that not only will government not help them, but also the government will take from them.

My hospice patients used to tell me all the time that they were terrified the government was going to come into their hollers and take their Bibles and guns.

How horrible to have lived in such a way to believe that the entire US government is against them. How horrendous to have to protect themselves from the very entities that are supposed to help out at times like this. How traumatizing to live in that reality, day in and day out.

# Day 26 of the Apocalypse
## Ground Zero, Gerton, NC, Pop. 301

Though it's too early to be certain, some estimates put the economic impact of Hurricane Helene as high as $200 billion, which would make it equally as costly as Katrina in US history. In these estimates, it's not clear to whom the storm is costly. Possibly the federal, state, and local governments, and disaster organizations. Most definitely to the people who lived in Helene's wake. In the midst of this deadly, devastating, expensive event, almost everyone we know, including Jeff and me, are getting turned down for financial help.

The Small Business Administration (SBA) called me recently to tell me they are out of money for any business who has applied for Economic Injury Disaster relief, which I did on October 4th. Specifically, the SBA states on its website that new loan offers will be delayed due to a "lapse in Congressional funding."

According to the SBA, Congress has to both be back in session and also agree to approve additional funds in order for the SBA to cover these loans. Congress will not reconvene until November 12th, six weeks following the hurricane.

Every single business that I know of in Western North Carolina is struggling. Tourism is gone in this area. Restaurants, that rely heavily on fourth quarter income to fund them for the rest of the year, are closed indefinitely.

For Congress to remain out of session, during a time when there is a federal disaster, is absurd. For our president to not enact his executive privilege to call Congress into session, is disgraceful.

The SBA has denied my application twice already. The first time because I did not meet a forty-eight-hour deadline. I had no internet or cell phone service at the time. The second time it was because they said I did not submit a specific IRS form they requested. On the SBA dashboard, I can see that I did in fact sign and submit that very form.

Yesterday we got turned down by our insurance company for a claim for destruction to our rainwater catchment system and our two-mile HOA road. We were told that because neither the system nor the road have anything to do with our house, they are not covered. The system cost $15,000 to install. The road will cost $30,000 to repair.

We also got billed by Duke Energy for this past month. The bill included the three weeks we had no power. It was the most expensive bill we have ever received from Duke.

We are not alone in this. Everyone we know is getting slapped with huge bills and being denied claims. To date, we haven't heard of FEMA covering any repairs for private roads, although many people we know have already tried to get assistance.

This is not a pity party for me or anyone else who is going through this. This is a wake-up call to see systemic issues. The very institutions that are supposed to be helping us at such a time as this are not helping. They are making it harder for us to thrive.

I can see even more clearly how conspiracy theories are perpetuated.

This is a harrowing experience, and Jeff and I are well resourced. We are able to qualify for loans. We have savings. We will have an income again once I start working with clients in January. There are many people who have lost their income or their home, or both. There is no hierarchy of suffering, but there is definitely a hierarchy of economic access.

## The Deep End of Hope in the Wake of Hurricane Helene

When there is no money, and no support...

When people have experienced devastating loss...

When people are mentally spent by trying to manage it all...

When they are living in the midst of trauma and destruction...

How do we lean in and move through it?

It is the people who don't assume money or support is on the way who are navigating this the best right now. Their lack of expectation is protecting their hearts and minds at this time. But their hearts were already hardened before this happened. They were traumatized well before Helene hit. They are living out a trauma response that has been going on for decades and generations. No one has ever helped them. They have never expected help. I'm beginning to understand this now.

Their solution is to figure it out on their own, just like they always have. They don't even expect to rely on the kindness of strangers. They just put their heads down and get through. For them, that is what life is about: getting through, not thriving.

Getting through is a coping mechanism. Thriving is a choice.

Regarding the SBA loan, I put on my big-girl pants and tried, once again, to advocate for myself. My friend Angie told me she knew someone connected with a small business center (SBC) in our area, who might be able to put me in touch with a business counselor. After several communications and applications with two different SBCs, I was finally connected with the right location in my county at the Blue Ridge Community College.

I got an intake call scheduled with a counselor named Ben. When I explained the situation to Ben about my application being once again rejected by the SBA, he told me he couldn't help me. That was in the first two minutes of our conversation. Already irritated, I was ready to get off of the phone.

Then Ben did something extraordinary. He started asking me what felt like eighty-five questions about my life and business. And he listened, deeply, to my answers. At first, I thought he was just being nosey. I didn't understand why he was asking if he couldn't help me.

Eventually, after telling him about my service as trauma chaplain, about my brothers dying, and about writing this book, I asked him why he wanted to know. See, I'm not one to go on and on about myself. At parties, it's my husband who does most of the talking. I am the quiet one in the background, taking it all in. I'm not usually center stage.

But I got real with Ben and just put it all out on the table, because what did I have to lose? He became very emotional and told me that when he woke up that morning, it was on his heart to really make a difference. God had told him to be of service.

Ben agreed to reach out to a contact of his at the SBA, to see about getting my application reopened. He also told me about a loan program for businesses here in Western North Carolina that I hadn't heard about that could be a great fit for my needs. He invited me to reach back out to him if I needed anything.

At the end of our call, he prayed for me. I hung up the phone and wept.

The next day I received a phone call from a woman named Desiree, at the Disaster Recovery Center for our county. She works for the SBA, and she offered to help me with my reapplication. I think Ben must have encouraged her to call me.

I got confused during our conversation, because she kept referring to "we." "We're going to go into your account and submit a letter of explanation." "We're going to submit the necessary forms."

I stopped her after a while, and said, Look, you've got to simplify things for me here. My brain isn't working the way it used to. Who is this 'we' that you keep referring to?" It never occurred to me that she would actually help me. After being turned down so many times in the past month from institutions that were designed to help, I had just about given up.

"Why, you and me, sweetie!" she replied, confused. "Who did you think I meant?" I had thought she meant I had to figure it out myself, and the "we" was my business and me.

I went to see Desiree the next day, at the Disaster Recovery Center. As promised, she helped me to reopen my SBA application. I started crying. Weeping, actually, the kind with snot running down my face and everything. My tears weren't really about the SBA application. They were all from my exhaustion, my grief, and my living in devastation, pouring out, uncontrollably.

Desiree hugged me hard and told me that it was going to be okay. She, too, prayed for me.

Recovery and healing are about being willing to make millions of decisions that may or may not work out. It's about having faith that the Universe has my back, and that more life is always possible. It's about taking that next step, even after all hope is lost. Ben and Desiree reminded me of these things, during a time when I had forgotten, after being rejected so many times.

Keep looking for evidence that things are working out. Keep looking for the helpers, like Mr. Rogers taught us all. Don't give up after the first no. This is about advocating for yourself, while *choosing* not to feel alone in the process.

I am trying the best I can. We are all trying the best we can, to make the next decision, and take the next step.

On the other side of this apocalypse, I want to thrive. I want to become a better version of myself. I want to be able to comfort myself when I am turned away by others. I want it to be easy to love myself and others in the midst of chaos. I want to keep advocating for myself, even when things don't seem to be working out.

I want to harden my heart, so the smallest of things doesn't bring me to a grinding halt, but not so much that I keep my head down and just get through. I want to be able to process what is happening in real time, so sorrow and grief don't get trapped in my body and in my heart. I want to heal as I go.

Humans are amazingly resilient creatures. I want to be fully human through this.

## Day 27 of the Apocalypse
### Ground Zero, Gerton, NC, Pop. 301

I had no idea when I married Jeff that we would live through a pandemic, an apocalypse, and multiple hard deaths in the first five years of our relationship.

There is no one I would rather be married to when shit gets real, y'all.

Jeff could have spent the past month just focused on the needs of our family, but instead he immediately began raising funds, coordinating supply deliveries for our community, and became the hub of communication for Gerton through his Facebook group, "We are Gerton, NC."

He did all of this while taking care of the two of us and Erik and Kate, and also cooking dinner every night for the four of us. He's up at 7:00 a.m. and doesn't go to bed until 1:00 or 2:00 a.m. most nights, ensuring that everyone has what they need.

Despite the cause, it has been an honor and a privilege seeing my husband in action in this way.

Aside from a few times that he's teared up when people showed up with extraordinary kindness, support, and resources, Jeff seems on the surface to be completely untraumatized by this event. I wonder if it's because he lived through Katrina. He knows what to expect. He understands the rhythm of disaster. He knows we are in this for the long haul. He also knows what's on the other side of this; he's already been through the internal and external reckoning process that some of us are just beginning to discover.

Jeff shared an example of his day in the "We are Gerton, NC" Facebook group a few weeks ago. It's stunning to read through it and see just how much he does in a single day:

"My day today:

"Woke up at 4:30 a.m. to the sound of my phone vibrating with incoming notifications—the first bit of cell coverage I've gotten in twenty-four hours.

"Spent two hours frantically trying to answer questions for this group along with the dozens of DMs from frantic family members (including my own), trying to locate their people or seeing if their property still exists.

"Slept thirty minutes and woke up to my 7:00 a.m. alarm. Turned on the generator for an hour so I could shower, charge everything, make a protein shake, and get my refrigerator/freezer a chance to keep what's left of our food from spoiling.

"Got dressed at 8:00 a.m.—turned off the generator and checked the propane gauge to see how many days we have left here in paradise (maybe twenty).

"Met my fearless/heroic fire rescue friend and neighbor and his badass team leader/chainsaw-wielding wife (also my friend) to start our three-mile hike down our 4,200-foot mountain.

"9:00 a.m. Reached the firehouse after walking what looks like a motor cross track followed by several stream crossings, while avoiding collapsing roadways and hitching a ride for the last half mile on the back of an ATV driven by an ER physician from SC and son of my neighbor who both drove up just to help (now friends).

"Attended the daily meeting where we learned who is trapped where, who needs food/water, what temporary bridge needs to be built today.

"9:30 a.m. Grabbed some supplies, hitched a ride from my ER-physician friend to the continental divide to take a shift manning a checkpoint designed to deter looters and other ne'r-do-wells from entering our Armageddon-like world and directed the multitude of selfless, brave volunteers and generous supply and construction equipment drivers where they needed to go.

"I also collected info from the outside world, like what grocery is open, what gas station is open (and takes cards) along with the bad news that just streams in constantly.

"12:00 p.m. My wife showed up at the checkpoint in a banana yellow Jeep with a 12" lift and 40" super swamper tires, having hitched a ride with a complete stranger who drove up from somewhere else to help us (now a friend). She has done the same hike I did by herself.

"12:45 p.m. Emma and I hitched a ride with a friend on the way back from the next town over that's pretty much as f'ed up as ours.

"1:00 p.m. Attended the town meeting where we tell everything we know to everyone that walked down to hear it. Emma gave a talk as our trauma chaplain offering her counseling services in our new PTSD-encrusted world. I ate some barbecue and offered advice as a Katrina survivor on how to navigate FEMA paperwork.

"2:00 p.m. Hitched a ride (with friends) back to my sentry post to take another shift as gatekeeper to the town. I used the breaks between cars and the limited cell signal there to attempt to buy a UTV that will help our old asses up and down our mountain. (Unsuccessfully: No voice calling available.)

"4:00 p.m. Hitched a ride with a random car I stopped at the checkpoint who turns out to be our former state representative.

"4:30 p.m. Back to the firehouse. Grabbed some snacks and some food stuffs, unloaded some new supplies that just came in, and tried desperately to catch a side-by-side driver to take us to our road's gate so we only have to hike one mile… straight up a mountain. We don't have much energy left.

"5:30 p.m. Got home, turned on the generator for three hours so we could shower, and wash clothes, and pretend that everything is like it was before.

"8:00 p.m. Met next door neighbors to hike up/down to our other neighbors' house to eat, tell stories, get drunk, and feel human.

"Home by 10:00 p.m. Let the dogs out, tucked my wife in, and here I am—answering questions for complete strangers (now friends) and typing this.

"What's my point?

"We all have a part to play. My day may not look like your day, but both were important. Tomorrow will be completely different. There are people who did a lot more than I did—heroic shit, but I did all I could, and so did they.

"Strangers become friends, and communities come together under extreme pressure. I love this place. I love these people. This is my home, and I will do my part to make it right. God bless us all."

# Day 28 of the Apocalypse
## Ground Zero, Gerton, NC, Pop. 301

My mother sent me notification of my brother Bryce's memorial, which is being held next month near Washington, DC. A square-shaped image, with his name, birth and death dates; his picture; and the date, time, and location of his memorial. A calming blue background holds the information together in a sorrowful yet appropriate way. I notice immediately that his last name is misspelled. Churchwood instead of Churchman.

He died over a week ago, and she and I still haven't had a conversation about his death. The three-minute conversation with her best friend is my closest connection to what happened. I don't call her, because she will make Bryce's death solely about her. I remain isolated in my grief, the last of us four still living.

This is the third of her three sons that she's organized a memorial for in the last three years. That is too much death, and too much life, to memorialize. Not catching this detail with his last name, which has also been her last name for fifty-seven years, is a trauma response. Details are one of the first things to go. The mind sees what it wants to see, instead of what is actually there.

In his photo, Bryce looks exactly like our father did at his age. Puffy rings under his eyes, a hallmark of too much alcohol over too long a period of time. Eyes which reveal the pain of loss, and missed opportunities, and grief. An untrimmed beard just beginning to grey. His mouth not even attempting a smile. Dad and Bryce both died at forty-eight.

The photo divulges more than I want to recall about Bryce. In my mind's eye, I still picture him as a young boy, playing with toy cars and homemade wooden blocks on the floor of his bedroom, making *vroom-vroom* noises, and of him happily living inside his own make-believe world.

I knew the ending of Bryce's life before it was even written. He knew it too. He called me the day our brother Alex died by suicide, two and a half months ago. Bryce was startling honest with me during that ten-minute conversation.

He told me that he didn't blame me for separating myself from our family so many years ago. He went on to disclose that he knew this was the only way I could protect myself, that it was okay that I was taking care of myself, that he was so glad I had a husband and a happy life. Alex told me the same thing in our last conversation, three weeks before he died.

Bryce also told me he always thought he would be the first of us to die. I responded immediately with, "I did, too."

I knew the drugs and alcohol would kill him after the first time he overdosed, when he was eleven years old, and I found him naked and strung out on the floor of his bedroom before school.

Even so, when I learned that he died from an overdose, my first thought was of that conversation we had only a few months ago. *Did my comment tip him over the edge? After all this time, was he waiting for me to tell him that I knew he would die?*

That is one detail that I will never know. I add it to my catalog of regrets.

Details matter. But just like our mother, I'm also missing so many of them right now. In fact, I am becoming immune to the details of the devastation surrounding me. They have become brown noise in the

## The Deep End of Hope in the Wake of Hurricane Helene

recesses of my mind. This is how I cope with living inside of them day in and day out.

Driving home from Asheville, I pass by piles of giant trees, trunks, and limbs, piled up haphazardly in yards or along the road, still littered with downed power lines. There is mud everywhere. It keeps sporadically raining here—not enough to cause more mudslides, but enough to keep a sheen of dirt on everything. We are surrounded by shades of brown.

I drive by a house that no longer has a roof and another one missing a side. Destruction and absence stand beside one another. I notice myself shying away from looking inside these homes at destroyed belongings. This is my way of protecting my neighbors' privacy and honoring their loss.

The highway parallels the creek-turned-river, which now houses crushed cars, trailers, and homes. The water keeps a steady pace, maneuvering its way around these objects.

The Baptist pastor drives past me in an excavator, cleaning up trash, which is everywhere. Along the roads, in yards, floating by in the river. *Storm debris* or *disaster debris* are the terms now used to explain this overwhelming proof of devastation.

If I pay too close attention, the debris might consume me, too.

Instead, I focus on what is new. Fresh gravel covering a muddy temporary road. Giant rocks filling in the gaps between the road and the driveways. A mailman, delivering mail on that new road.

I don't know how my life will end, just like I don't know what my world will look like a year or five years from now.

I hope it will look like our community still coming together and doing what we need to, in order to support each other. I hope our hearts and homes will be rebuilt.

I hope that when I drive through our community, I will no longer feel the need to protect myself from the devastation, because I will be surrounded by fiercely protected life.

## Day 29 of the Apocalypse
Ground Zero, Gerton, NC, Pop. 301

There are six "camps" of people who have revealed themselves during this apocalypse. I call them Evacuees, Helpers, Donors, Preppers, Looters, and Homesteaders. These categories can really apply to any horrendous situation, whether that is in the confines of a family, corporation, or a natural disaster.

It takes all kinds of people to make a community. There is no judgment in my evaluation of how people have chosen to respond. It is completely understandable that people do what they need to do to take care of themselves. Everyone is doing the best that they can—the best they know how—during an extraordinarily difficult time.

The Evacuees left our area as quickly as possible. They saw the writing on the wall: This was not going to be an easy fix. Some got out to save themselves, either by helicopter or by finding their own way out. Some left because they knew they would be a burden and didn't want to draw on resources. Some of them are relocating permanently. Others plan to be away for six months to a year, until their homes or properties become inhabitable.

The Helpers saw the extent of the devastation, took an inventory of their skill sets, and immediately stepped in to assist, wanting to ensure our community was safe and protected.

For example, our friend Brock, who couldn't get to work after the hurricane because his road washed away, built a new road in a location that was deemed impassable to allow access for his entire neighborhood. Our next-door neighbor and first responder Erik, who saved a man and his dog who were buried in mud up to their chests. Or my husband, Jeff, who is still coordinating supply donations and communication.

These are just things that people did before outside help showed up. Some people stepped up and became the solution. Some went into overdrive with helping, and worked nonstop, sixteen-hour days, until our fire chief told them take a mandatory day or week off. You can't help when you are overly exhausted and strung out.

Some local Helpers are still showing up, even though it's been a month, and lots of outside help has since intervened. They are playing the long game and are committed to building this brave new world.

The Donors are a group of people who live here, but either weren't here when the hurricane hit, or have second homes here. They gave generously, and often, with resources, supplies, and financial donations. Our closest neighbors each allowed us to "raid" their homes for anything we could need. One of them even offered their sheets and towels, in case we weren't able to do laundry.

Donors drove to Gerton from as far away as Florida and delivered gas, Starlink systems, generators, vegan food (for Kate), alcohol (which you already know was very much appreciated), and love. Some donors are complete strangers we have never met and will probably never meet. They Venmoed and mailed financial support to us and our community for their own reasons. We are grateful to all of them.

The Preppers came into their heyday right from Day 1. They have anticipated an apocalypse for decades; even longed for it. Their homes are fully stocked with food. They have generators and wells. Some of them even have solar power. All of them have a variety of weapons. Many of them, who have lived here for their whole lives, already live off-grid. They are mountain people who know how to take care of themselves.

The Preppers eagerly embraced the devastation and collapse of society as we know it and have been oddly invigorated and calm through this whole experience. Or perhaps they are calm because they haven't really noticed a big change in their own lifestyle. Their eccentric commentary and lifestyle are what has made them the most resilient camp.

Looting became a legitimate concern early on, with people coming into Gerton to pillage homes and businesses. Even some people within our community began doing this on Day 1. It was like the Wild West here during the first few weeks, chaotic and lawless. Some people had the attitude that they should just take everything they could, because there was no way to know when more would show up. A couple of Airbnb guests from Florida looted Bearwallow Provision Company on Day 1, robbing the owner of merchandise that his insurance company will not reimburse because there is no evidence of it ever existing. I get it, they were concerned, because they probably had no food in their rental house. They weren't able to think about anything beyond their own primal needs. These are the Looters.

A lot of people wanted to stay because of the lawlessness. They wanted to protect what is theirs. They refused to be evacuated. Or they didn't have money to evacuate. These people remained even though they shouldn't have, because their homes were damaged and mold was growing on the walls or because they didn't have generators, or water, or their roads were gone. These are the Homesteaders.

A significant portion of our resources went toward attending to some of the Homesteaders during the first month. They couldn't get from their homes to the fire station to collect supplies or get hot meals, so every day, twice a day, food and supplies had to be taken to them. Some of them needed medical attention, like having new oxygen tanks brought to them each day because each tank only lasted for four hours. Instead of the majority of our help and resources being given to searching for missing people and clearing trees and rebuilding roads so we could get power restored, we instead had to prioritize keeping a significant number of people fed and resourced. We had to help the few instead of the many. This was hard to swallow for all of us, because there was so much work to be done for our entire community to be able to function.

But this is always what happens during a disaster.

The common denominator of all of the people who stayed though, regardless of their participation or burden, is that there is no time for emotional response right now.

Emotions were there the first couple of weeks, with tears and frustration. Now they are gone, and in that vacuum a deadening has surfaced.

For example, people who fled or who had second homes here are starting to reappear. They are so upset by the devastation, although to us it looks much better than it did on Day 1, because we have things like power and temporary roads now.

These people with fresh eyes are filled with emotion, wanting to talk through everything. Their energy is frenetic. They are inconsolable. We nod and smile but can't really soothe them.

We are like walking dead people, devoid of emotion. It's not callousness for us. It's our new way of existing.

This is a trauma response. If we were to really feel the reality that we are now living in, we wouldn't be able to function. It's a funky version of fight, flight, or freeze. We've shut down the parts of us that aren't necessary for basic operations. We still can eat, shit, and sleep. We still can have basic conversations. We're even able to engage pretty well with things not related to the emotionality of the apocalypse. We look human, and act human, with this one exception.

There is no emotional landscape for our current reality.

This is unspoken among those of us who stayed. We don't sit around analyzing our lack of emotional response to the apocalypse. It's just a given, a way of life for us right now.

This is resilience in action. This is what you do when there isn't the luxury of self-care or being nonfunctional.

Jeff has always been this way, resilient and unemotional when he is asked to pivot and change directions. I didn't understand until now how he can be such a fantastic communicator, with access to his emotions, but when it comes to living life and navigating unexpected change, he has a certain attitude that has always confused me. He just does what is needed to do to get through. It's a "suck up and deal" kind of attitude, mixed with startling confusion about why it might be hard for me to change on a dime.

During Hurricane Katrina, Jeff's house flooded on the ground floor. He had to evacuate his family to another state. Jeff stayed in New Orleans, living in a trailer next to temporary offices for the medical company he was working for. The vibe of New Orleans changed drastically. Overnight there was mass looting and rampant violence. He responded by trading in his sports car and buying a Hummer and learning to always have a gun on him for protection. Jeff was forced to live in a very dangerous situation for a year, before his home was fixed and his family could return. Still today he doesn't use turn signals when driving, because in the wake of Katrina he discovered that when he did, people were more likely to follow him and try to hijack him.

It's nearly twenty years later, and Jeff is still operating on the defensive. He is either always prepared or immediately upset that he wasn't already prepared. This was part of the impetus for buying a UTV, so we will never again be unprepared, stuck, or trapped.

The UTV epitomizes how Jeff is processing this trauma. He processes by preparing. Over the past two weeks, I have watched Jeff diligently accessorize our new UTV. It is quickly becoming the ultimate off-road vehicle.

Two three-foot-tall, thin, bright red gas canisters have been adhered to each side of the two-person side-by-side. There are now mirrors on both sides of the vehicle, as well as a long rearview mirror, to enhance our ability to see around us when we are driving up and down our mountain to the main road. There is an interior magnetic light, so that at night we can see the ignition.

Yesterday he added grab handles for both the driver and passenger, placing them parallel to the rearview mirror, so that we can reach up and hold on when the road gets bumpy. All of our roads are super bumpy now. Jeff also added a round knob for the wheel, so that it's easier to turn the vehicle, especially when reversing.

Then there's the fire extinguisher, first aid kit, and ham radio system he added. The latter required him taking multiple trips around our fire district, to test the distance of the radio system. I dutifully waited at home by two walkie talkies, set to two different stations, responding every five minutes to his messages of "Emma, are you there?" and "Click three times if you can hear me." Not being able to communicate after the hurricane was terrifying. For that reason Jeff is getting his ham radio license.

Today he has moved to the back of the UTV, adding an extender to the back bed, to increase how much we can carry. His next move is to install a bench that rests toward the back of the bed, directly behind where the driver and passenger sit, where Erik and Kate can sit when we travel together.

Jeff has also hand-washed the UTV, twice, and completed its first oil change, as we logged so many hours on it already.

I do not believe it is physically possible to add any more accessories to this vehicle, but where there is a will, there is a way, and I know that Jeff will prevail if he believes it is possible and necessary. In fact, he's already hinting that the UTV "needs" taller tires for more ground clearance.

For Jeff, preparation is his way through trauma. That is true for many of us. There is a gift in being able to harden our hearts. We are able to be resilient and in action. We are able to wake up each morning and function in our war zone.

I am doing this very same thing right now, through writing this book. If I can write my way through the apocalypse, maybe, eventually, I can make sense of it, to myself and others.

This is not callousness. It's a reorientation. It's a different way of viewing the world. Things that used to be so very important to focus on have lost their grip.

There was who we were before the flood. And who we are now, after the flood. We're not putting on brave faces and pretending to be okay. We're simply rewired. A setting in our DNA has forever changed.

It's like one day I am shopping at Whole Foods, complaining about people's attitudes, and the next day I'm living in our version of a war zone. Priorities change real fast.

Santa Claus is climbing back up the chimney. The Tooth Fairy has run out of money. We now live in a devastated world.

## Day 30 of the Apocalypse
### Ground Zero, Gerton, NC, Pop. 301

There is a name for how many people have responded in the wake of Helene. It is called *catastrophe compassion.*

Catastrophe compassion is widespread and consistent across disasters. It follows war, terrorist attacks, natural disasters such as earthquakes, hurricanes, tsunamis, the COVID-19 pandemic, and in our case, an apocalypse.

It is how people respond in the wake of crisis.

For decades, social scientists have documented two primary narratives about human behavior during crises. The first narrative states that following disasters, individuals either panic, ignore social order, or act selfishly.

Popular media prefers to focus on panic and cruelty, like after Hurricane Katrina when violence ensued. In fact, *The New York Times* described the city as a "snake pit of anarchy, death, looting, raping, marauding thugs."[6] Stories like this informed New Orleans's response to this crisis. The National Guard was called in to "take control" of the city, rather than focusing on humanitarian relief.

---

[6] https://www.nytimes.com/2005/09/03/opinion/united-states-of-shame.html

It is true that when there is an emergency, social order breaks down.

You can't trust a human who is trying to get basic needs met, to make spiritually advanced decisions. This is what makes us the "killer monkey." If you are not awakened to the greater accountability of humanity, then you become reduced to the animalistic behavior of doing whatever it takes to survive.

Jeff lived through this in New Orleans during Katrina. Hurricanes were not new in New Orleans, but this was the first hurricane that brought what had been promised for hundreds of years: total annihilation.

The flood waters were eight or even twelve feet deep in some areas. People who didn't have anything started seeking higher ground, along with materials and supplies. There were a lot of people who had nothing to begin with and who couldn't get out of New Orleans to seek refuge. Meanwhile, no one could get in to help them, either.

Many people were used to going to the grocery store every day, because they didn't have space to keep stored food or didn't have money to buy large quantities of food. They had minimal supplies on hand and were desperate for food and water. Of course it made sense that these people looted homes and stores. This was necessary vandalism.

There were abandoned cars blocking roads. Jeff and his neighbors broke many car windows and steering locks to push cars off to the side of the roads in their neighborhood so emergency services could get through. This was also necessary vandalism.

Jeff remembers that some people, however, were opportunists. They took advantage of the chaos and lawlessness and looted nonessentials like televisions. In Jeff's narrative, the police all left the city during the flooding. There was no one to stop the roving bands of looters walking the streets. Then the National Guard came in and the looting ending.

But lawlessness is only a small part of the disaster response.

The second, larger narrative comes from historical records. These records don't depict people as antisocial and savage. Rather they

# The Deep End of Hope in the Wake of Hurricane Helene

showcase prosocial behavior and feelings of community. They speak of disparate people coming together in extraordinary ways. Disaster survivors develop communities with widespread acts of altruism and mutual aid. They experience a heightened sense of solidarity.

This also happened during Katrina. Jeff remembers that everyone needed help getting their refrigerators out of their houses. The power was out for months, and they were full of maggots and rotting food. People walking down the street would be called in to help move heavy fridges out of homes. It's just what was done to help.

Neighbors also worked together to organize storm debris for removal. One of Jeff's neighbors, a pharmaceutical rep, had serious medicine samples lying all over the ground outside her house, following the flooding. He and other neighbors picked them up and disposed of them safely.

That feeling of community happened here in Gerton as well. People who Jeff and I only knew in passing have become close friends. Others we had never interacted with are now called often. We regularly end our conversations by saying "I love you." We miss each other when we don't talk every day. We grieve, as our community begins to fall back into its daily grind, and people no longer show up at the fire station to check in.

There is a camaraderie and a deep knowing when we speak to people who have been through this disaster with us. It is the common language of surviving, coupled with a new capacity to exist. It is a trust, knowing that whatever happens in the future, we will have each other's backs.

Anytime one of our neighbors reaches out asking for help, we say yes. That is our common refrain now, "Yes." Yes, we are willing. Yes, we can help. Yes, we are here for you. Yes, we will do whatever it takes to make your life better or easier, if only for a few moments.

Many of us look back on the early days following Helene with nostalgia. This is common among "disaster survivors." Floods, bombings, and earthquakes are horrific, but offer a level of interdependence and altruism difficult to find during normal times. We miss being in community, and in communion, with one another.

Catastrophe compassion doesn't only have to exist during disasters. It can be for every day, too.

## Day 31 of the Apocalypse
Ground Zero, Gerton, NC, Pop. 301

There are many people who want to help following a crisis. Unaffected people descend on scenes of disasters to volunteer, flooding them with donations and willing hands. This is a phenomenon known as *disaster convergence*.

Our area has definitely experienced its fair share of disaster convergence. We've had hundreds of volunteers come to Gerton over the past month. Some simply dropped off very needed supplies, and then left, understanding they would just get in the way.

Some stayed, and brought with them their own ATV transportation, equipment, and set of skills. They slept in tents, trailers, or campers they brought. Many brought their own food, so as to avoid adding a burden. They offered a phenomenal amount of help, assisting with everything from very technical work to boring work, like reorganizing supplies. They always said yes when asked to help. These volunteers who truly wanted to help, found a way to help, without question or complaint.

Others showed up unresourced and unskilled.

We witnessed a number of volunteers getting upset when we didn't immediately have something for them to do or when we weren't as organized as they wanted us to be. Many brought absolutely no skills other than "willing hands," and were turned away. We patiently listened to them when they told us how frustrating it was for them to have driven so long to get to us, only to be turned away.

A few volunteers had specific ideas of what they wanted to do that were not accommodated. They wanted to heroically ride on a side-by-side (that they *did not* bring themselves) to a collapsed home to rescue a trapped family. When, instead, they were asked to organize supplies, they got upset. These volunteers fall into another part of the overarching umbrella of disaster convergence. These are people who say to themselves, "I feel good when I help these poor people." That is pity, not compassion. That is acting from self-gratification.

There is another phenomenon called *clout chasing*. A clout chaser is a person or group of people who want to attain fame by putting themselves in proximity with someone, or something, that can leverage their fame.

We had a group of volunteers show up here in Gerton with six mules, wanting to "help." The mules clogged up our fire station parking lot an entire afternoon, shitting everywhere, and causing first responders to not be able to gather and check in with our chief. The volunteers wanted a mission to "save people."

Eventually they decided to transport four five-gallon containers of diesel fuel over the mountain to Middle Fork. This mission could have been accomplished in a much shorter amount of time by one volunteer with a UTV. But the mule volunteers insisted.

So Erik gave them very explicit instructions about how to get over the mountain, and they took off. At 11:00 p.m., they radioed the station, asking to be rescued, because they were lost. Firefighters then had to go out in the middle of the night and help get them off the mountain. They never did deliver the diesel fuel. They were clout chasers, pulling on our much needed resources, for their own benefit.

Other people showed up to "volunteer," with cameras in tow. Vloggers and YouTubers talked into their cameras the entire time they were here. They wandered around our community, taking photos without permission, of devastated homes, full of private possessions.

We didn't ask people to show up here. We did not invite them. They invited themselves. It is not helpful to come into a devastated community and make the situation about you.

Short-term missions have become popular in the wake of disasters. Often with little preparation, no knowledge of local culture (or sometimes even language), an absence of coordination with government officials, and no plans for long-term follow-up, volunteers show up in droves to "help." Without technical skills, resources, or a way to take care of themselves, they become just another burden to people who are living in the disaster.

I add myself to this list of people with willing hands. I spent a month in Kenya in 2011, and I traveled in the ministry, speaking to groups of Quakers. I volunteered for a week in a rural hospital. I ended up helping to paint the surgery wing because that was the only activity hospital staff could find for us to do with our "willing hands." I know, deep in my heart, that I was also a burden to that community, with my inability to speak the local dialect and my limited skills.

Part of me didn't want to write about volunteerism at all, because I know this will upset people. I know there are people with big hearts and willing hands, who truly want to make a difference. All I am suggesting is that when considering what it means to make a difference, take into account the people *needing* help, the situations they are surviving, or how to contribute, specifically. If that is not clear, maybe showing up with helping hands isn't the right thing to do.

I'm inviting all of us to consider what it truly means to be compassionate. Compassion arises from a sense of shared humanity, from solidarity, respect, and a profound awareness of interconnectedness.

The underlying human impetus is to want to help. We are more inclined to help when we identify with the people who are suffering. Each of us identifies with multiple groups, based on our race, upbringing, generation, ideology, or profession. It is easy for us to express loyalty, care, and pro-sociality toward members of our own groups. In the wake of Helene, many people who came here identified with the people of Western North Carolina. They could see themselves in us.

Emotional connection can also motivate disaster convergence and catastrophe compassion. When we share in, understand, and care for the emotional experience of others, we want to reach out and help. I experienced this when my brother died two weeks after the hurricane. This disaster upon disaster claimed people's hearts. There was an extraordinary outpouring of love and support for me, from hundreds of people who I don't know personally. They shared their own vulnerable stories of suicide with me.

Disasters lower psychological barriers and create immediate opportunities for connection and community. Compassion is immediately available. Disasters trigger a deep sense of vulnerability. We are brought together in our grief, our disorientation, and our disbelief, whether we are living in the disaster or observing it from the outside.

In the highest form of compassion, we are aware that suffering exists, we are empathetic to it, and we are committed to alleviating the suffering that accompanies it. Disasters offer us the opportunity to do all three of these things.

Our opportunity, as a people, is to learn how to do this when there is no disaster.

# Day 32 of the Apocalypse
## Ground Zero, Gerton, NC, Pop. 301

In the wake of disaster, legends are created.

There are stories of heroes, like one we heard about from Bat Cave: a mysterious Australian Airbnb guest, who appears at exactly the right time. An eight-year-old boy is trapped under a house that slid off its foundation and landed in what used to be the highway. The Australian somehow locates a carjack (in the woods), jacks up the house, and pulls the boy out from under the house. The Australian is never seen or heard from again.

This is a phenomenon that happens in disasters. Strange people show up at exactly the right time, and perform miracles, then are never seen again.

Later we confirm that it was actually Rich, a Brit who saved that nine-year-old girl trapped in her house on Day 1, but I like the legend, too.

Then there are stories that make you shake your head and wonder if they were even possible. But they stick in your mind, a reminder of the cost of devastation.

There were people who rode out the storm in their homes that were washed off of their foundations by flooding and mudslides. A washed-out house is now stranded, in the midst of rubble, covering what used to be a highway. An elderly woman is found inside the crumpled home, sitting in a recliner in the corner of her living room. There is mud everywhere. The sliding glass doors are off their tracks and open to the outdoors. A flipped over couch blocks entrance from the doors, so "bears can't get in."

The woman is in her pajamas and slippers, with the recliner slightly inclined. She is surrounded by furniture and other objects that moved as the house was pushed down the road by water.

She is cheerful when strangers arrive to help her. They tell her they are there to rescue her. Her reply: "I don't need to be rescued, I just need help moving things away from my chair." She had hip replacement surgery a few weeks prior and is having trouble getting around. "I'm fine," she says, "Please just move my recliner six inches back so I can raise my feet higher."

The woman seems undisturbed by the mud, broken doors, and her household being in shambles and off of its foundation.

The strangers go to move items back into place. One of them starts to move a large ornamental flower vase from the floor next to the woman that has some kind of liquid in it sloshing around. The woman cries out, "No, baby, don't move that! That's where I've been going to the bathroom."

Like all of us, this woman was just doing what she needed to do, to get by. But it was too late, the stench was everywhere.

Years from now, it is stories like these—the miraculous and the unbelievable—that we will remember the most.

The Concert for Carolina, which took place this week, will also become legendary. It's a tale of musicians coming together in support of North and South Carolina, in the wake of a devastating hurricane.

A record number of people were in attendance: 82,193. The concert raised $24.5 million for North and South Carolina. All proceeds will be split between nonprofits supported by musicians Luke Combs and Eric Church, including the Chief Cares Fund, Samaritan's Purse,

## The Deep End of Hope in the Wake of Hurricane Helene

Manna Food Bank, Second Harvest Food Bank of Northwest North Carolina, and Eblen Charities.

Eric Church also pledged to build one hundred new homes for displaced people in Avery County, through his organization Chief Cares.

Chase Rice, another musician, grew up in nearby Fairview. He spoke about Craigtown. This is an area of Fairview where nine Craig family members died in mudslides, as did firefighter Tony Garrison and his nephew, who were trying to save them. Luke Combs also attended high school in Fairview.

Jeff and I wanted to watch the concert when we arrived home from the beach. But figuring out how to claim our free ticket, and then getting the concert to broadcast live on our television was too much for our hurricane brains to figure out.

We also arrived home to heavy rain and wind, the first rain in thirty days. I think it would have been okay if it was only rain, but the addition of wind was too reminiscent of the hurricane.

So, after we unpacked the car, I put myself to bed and slept for ten hours, my new normal.

It's been a month since Hurricane Helene devastated our community, and two weeks since my brother died.

Grief is stretching me. So is gratitude.

I got a voice message from FEMA last week asking me if we had sustained damage to a private well or private bridge, which makes me wonder if they are now considering covering those recovery costs.

Our county put out a survey asking about damage to private roads, which makes me wonder if they, too, are considering covering those recovery costs.

The most remote area of our fire district, Middle Fork, is getting their power restored this weekend.

Our friends Brandon and Mackenzie are hosting a Halloween party and trick or treating for kids and adults in our community on October 31st.

We still have an abundance of supplies at our fire station.

As the reality of this 30,000-year geological event is becoming realized, help and possibility are showing up in unexpected ways.

Jeff and I believe that what we focus on expands. So we're focusing on abundance and this brave new world that we're creating in the wake of this experience. As Jeff regularly reminds me, everything always works out for us. Our job is to believe and keep showing up.

# Reflections on Trauma in the Reconstruction Phase

In the reconstruction phase, the PTSD disaster symptoms have fully set in. The people experiencing them are now paying attention and wondering what is wrong with them.

The most common symptom I saw was people having trouble falling asleep or staying asleep. Numbness was prevalent for many people, including Jeff and me. We became immune to our own emotions and to the emotions of others.

Everyone we know had a hard time concentrating or getting their brains to work properly. The simplest of tasks felt overwhelming, because our body or brain memory of how to do something wasn't accessible.

When the adrenaline finally slowed, which took two to three weeks for most of us on the ground, body pain set in. We started to feel the bruises all over our bodies from all the bushwhacking and hauling supplies. My migraines increased to being an almost daily occurrence.

Exhaustion also set in, and many of us walked around like zombies, never able to get enough rest to feel rested. Our bodies were attempting to heal themselves through rest.

It became challenging to hear others' trauma stories or even to share our own. We went from eagerly repeating our stories to one another over the first few weeks, to not wanting to talk at all about what happened. When we finally had contact with the outside world, we didn't want to discuss what had happened.

Reliving those stories became another form of trauma.

Some of us had baggage with the people we ended up helping. Reconstruction looks like working through that emotionally in the aftermath of just doing what needed to be done, without bringing emotions into it.

Many people thought they were alone in these experiences. My chaplaincy work became the simple practice of normalizing symptoms.

Many of these symptoms occurred not only because we were living in a devastated world, but because we cannot equip the heart for mass destruction and devastation.

When devastation comes, who people were before the disaster will directly inform how they function after. If they assume the world is out to get them, that will be their experience in the wake of the disaster. If they know in their hearts that they are divinely guided, and divinely protected, that, too, will become the experience. A person's orientation to themselves and the world dictates how they navigate devastation.

We all deserve, and need, comfort and support in the wake of disaster.

I did a bunch of research on "helpful steps for adults after a disaster," the majority of which annoyed me.

There were a lot of suggestions to exercise, which lacks the understanding that our bodies were so physically overworked during the first month, exercise was impossible.

Many recommended limiting exposure to the disaster. I can see the benefit of not scrolling through social media, or reading too many articles, or looking at too many pictures and videos. But when you live in the devastation and have to drive or walk through it in order to get anywhere, that advice also isn't helpful.

What would be more helpful is the advice to *choose* what to focus on. I began focusing on things like sections of the road being repaired or trees being removed or speaking with the guy who was directing traffic on closed roads and learning his story. Focusing on new life and new possibility helped me.

The disaster advice I read recommended using credible sources of information to avoid speculation and rumors. This I absolutely agree with. I did notice that some people had a predilection to exaggerate or create rumors about things. This caused strain and stress in our community. These people may have been having a stress-response themselves and may not have been able to be present with what was really happening. Albeit unintentional, their stress caused other people to be more upset than necessary. Paying attention to that drama wasn't helpful.

Meditating, practicing mindfulness, and breathing exercises also made the top of the list of things "disaster victims should be doing." These, too, felt unattainable, but listening to music was possible for me. Listening to music is not something that requires conscious thought; it's something we can simply take in. I also got a massage, which was incredibly helpful for soothing my body and reminding me that my body wasn't the enemy in this "war zone" we're living in.

A client of mine recommended tapping (Emotional Freedom Technique). This worked well for me, because I could use it anywhere, anytime, and she gave me very simple instructions of where and how to tap: "imagine your hands are butterfly wings and tap the wings on your collarbone." Tapping points are similar to those used in acupuncture. Tapping on specific points on the body helps manage emotions and reduce stress.

Eating well, limiting alcohol and other substance consumption, and hydrating were on every disaster recovery list. We definitely drank too much alcohol the first few weeks. I did notice a difference when I intentionally stopped pouring myself a glass of wine at dinner. Most of us were also severely dehydrated. We could never get enough water or electrolytes in us, to get us peeing every hour, or whatever the measurement is for hydration. I still have to remind myself to drink more, when prior to the hurricane I was always well-hydrated.

Engaging in fun activities and staying connected with people was helpful advice. We spend a lot of time with our different neighbors, sharing meals, or watching movies, or just catching up on the latest gossip. This creates moments of normalcy in our world.

The catch-all advice still applies to remind self and others that it's normal to have many different feelings, as well as good days and bad days, as a natural part of recovery.

Then of course there is the advice to seek out mental health support, if the distress remains high after several weeks to a month, if you are having persistent trouble functioning at work or home, or if you are thinking about hurting yourself or someone else.

There is no judgment here of how you are responding.

Every day is a new day. Every day all anyone needs to do is to show up to the best of their ability, even if that means staying in bed, in jammies, with the dogs, and watching silly movies.

During this period of reconstruction, this was the prayer that came to me:

> Loving God, our minds, bodies, and spirits feel tired and worn down.
>
> Give us strength. Restore us.
>
> When things feel impossible, show us that all things are possible with you.
>
> Holy God we pause and pay attention to you and to everything that is.
>
> Awaken our souls to the sound of your whisper.
>
> Gently lead us onward out into the future.

### The Deep End of Hope in the Wake of Hurricane Helene

Grant us all to be the best we can at being human,

And as we try, make us in our trying holy, as you are Holy.

Hear our prayers, from our lips and from the beat of our hearts.

Grant us the strength and wisdom to reconstruct, through faith and gratitude, and through your Divine presence.

In your name we pray, Amen.

# PART 4
# EVOLUTION

# Day 33 of the Apocalypse
## Ground Zero, Gerton, NC, Pop. 301

My personality is not apocalyptic. I don't "worst case scenario" my way through life. Nor am I a glass-half-empty kind of person. In fact, I generally assume things will work out for me, even during times when that seems physically or logistically impossible.

For the most part, things do work out for me. Especially when my ego and I get out of the way. Especially when my focus is on saying YES to how God is leading me.

This is not normal behavior in our world.

But neither is "prepping," and planning for the "inevitable end of the world."

The Preppers are right. We can never be prepared enough for the unknown.

I'm right, too. Because at the end of the day, regardless of what happens, what will make or break a person is attitude and perspective.

When your home, your possessions, your land, your community, your societal infrastructure, your connection to the outside world, and the people who you love are all gone in a matter of hours, what will you have left?

What are you made of, without any of this? What is your identity and your role in this brave new world?

We have run out of time for you to figure this out. Things are speeding up. Those of you who are sensitive have been feeling this for years.

I am not apocalyptic. I am not a Prepper. But in the wake of Helene, I have become fiercely present. Paying attention in this way has shown me that we will continue to face more frequent natural disasters and political and societal breakdowns in the coming years.

That is the cost of being human at this time. Our opportunity lies in learning how to process trauma *as* we are going through it.

That is part of my impetus in writing this: To give witness to my own process with the trauma of Helene, as well as my brothers' suicides, in real time, and to show how others around me are coping with their own trauma.

The days of being able to spend a decade on a therapist's couch exploring your feelings are over. We must learn how to process as we go. If I can do this, you can too.

## Day 34 of the Apocalypse
## Ground Zero, Gerton, NC, Pop. 301

I've been craving normal—a normal routine, a normal schedule, a normal reality—which isn't really possible right now, but sometimes I can find moments of normalcy.

There's a walk/hike I normally do every day, using a combination of gravel roads and paths through our eighty-five-acre HOA. It's a walk, because I stroll leisurely, but also a hike, because there's about a 600-foot elevation gain.

The dogs and I haven't done this walk/hike since before the hurricane. Initially, all of my hiking was devoted to getting down and up the mountain, three miles each way, to be able to get to the fire station when there was no road access. Road access arrived on Day 12, when the thirty-foot chasm that was our connecting road was replaced by a temporary, narrow, one-lane road. Then our UTV arrived on Day 14, which made getting around anywhere easier.

Once we had our UTV, my body stopped cooperating. My adrenaline slowed down, and I no longer had the bandwidth to hike, exercise, or do much of anything beyond getting basic needs met.

Now, two weeks later, I want to get back to my normal exercise and movement routine, because my body is in constant pain (thanks to chronic Lyme disease), and I know movement helps. So does sleeping, eating right, and not living in an apocalypse. I'm managing what I can and letting the rest go.

By this afternoon the foggy morning turned into a brilliant sunny day, around 65 degrees, perfect for a walk/hike. The dogs were eager to "go for walkies," and immediately took off down the trail behind our house. Leaves are now covering all the roads, hiding the gaps and gashes left by the hurricane. They even cover some of the tree branches that were haphazardly moved to the side of the road weeks ago, in an effort to get vehicles through as soon as possible.

Our walk/hike takes about an hour, and halfway through brings us to the highest point in our neighborhood, a crest in the mountaintop overlooking the wide swath of mountains below us. We call it the "sit spot," because years ago Jeff and I hauled a bench up there, so I would have a place to sit, meditate, pray, and listen.

The path leading up to the sit spot is clear of debris, which makes me think that our neighbor Walter, when he visited from Charleston last week, must have driven his ATV up to the path to clear trees. He likes the sit spot, too.

I am deep in thought by this part of our walk/hike. The dogs are busy smelling everything, dutifully searching through the fallen leaves for bear poop, deer poop, coyote poop, other-dog poop, or really any form of poop to eat. I never get that part about dachshunds. *What is so appealing about smelling and eating someone else's poop?*

When I finally look up, at the top of the path, what I see takes my breath away. What I should have seen was a little circle of trees, a path around them, and our bench on the far side of the trees. Instead, there is a gaping cavern of nothingness but fallen trees and mud. A gigantic mudslide has swept the entire crest of the mountain away.

The path is gone. So is the bench. To the right of me is a three-story-high gash in the mountain exposing a muddy rock wall. I can't even tell by looking at the cavern where the bench should have been.

## The Deep End of Hope in the Wake of Hurricane Helene

It never occurred to me that Mother Nature would have touched this sacred place. She had protected the Baptist church in Gerton, as well as the churches in nearby Bat Cave and Chimney Rock. Why would she annihilate my outdoor church?

So much was washed away by the hurricane. So many sacred things taken. But this has always been the state of the natural world. After devastation, new life is formed. Nature knows how to bounce back much better than humans.

On our walk/hike back to the house we see wild turkeys roaming and evidence of both deer and bear walking on the roads. We hear so many birds flitting around in the trees above us and squirrels and chipmunks scampering through the leaves below. All these animals have found a way to keep living in this brave new world, where so much has been cleansed and stripped of its original design.

Nature abhors a vacuum. Every space is meant to be filled. The animals have already started doing this. Our role now as humans is to find ways to create our own sense of fullness.

Fullness begins with gratitude.

I was able to walk/hike with my dogs on a beautiful fall day. With so many trees gone, our mountain views are even more prominent.

I am safe.

I am warm.

I am fed.

I am loved.

I am able to love others.

I am always cared for. I am always supported. Things always work out, even when that looks radically different from what I would have imagined.

The giant cavern is making room for something new to show up.

# Day 35 of the Apocalypse
## Ground Zero, Gerton, NC, Pop. 301

There's a homeless dog that has been wandering around since the storm. He is reddish brown, fifty or sixty pounds, middle-aged, and may be a black mouth cur. His ears are darker than the rest of him, and he is stocky in stature.

The dog has moved impressive distances—probably no more than a fifteen-mile radius, but up and down multiple mountains, crossing creeks and destroyed roads. Every day he's in a new place.

People have been posting photos of him in various local Facebook groups. Jeff put out a call for help in his "We are Gerton, NC" Facebook group, since he is showing up in Gerton multiple times a week. People responded immediately.

The dog has made it as far south as Lake Lure, and as far north as Fairview. No one has stepped up to claim him. We don't know if his owners aren't on social media or were killed in a mudslide or evacuated without him. He's got no collar or identification on him. We do know he likes fire stations and churches, as those are the places he frequents.

This dog is super skittish and very, very smart. No one, despite radical efforts, has been able to catch him. Yesterday our friend Jamie finally managed to get a leash around his neck (a first!), while someone else distracted him with food, but the dog still got away.

The good news is that he's finally begun to accept food. In fact, we now know his favorites are cat food and chicken. Lots of people are feeding him. Someone even donated money via my husband to ensure he has enough food to eat.

Last week someone on Facebook named him Gert. Now every time a person sees him, they call out "Gert!" expecting him to magically understand that he's been renamed by an entire population.

Three months ago, things would have been much different for this dog. There would have been an irritated post on Facebook from someone saying a dog kept showing up in their yard.

Commenters would have suggested calling animal control or a local shelter to come and deal with him. Or, better yet, would have accused the person making the post of being irresponsible, for not having already taken those steps.

In the wake of Hurricane Helene, there are now hour-by-hour posts with sightings of Gert in different neighborhoods. People volunteer dog crates or specialty leashes to catch Gert. Many people take turns watching for him to walk by. Others announce what kind of food they gave him, and at what time, perhaps so his menu remains varied, or so others know when he last ate.

Gert is one of thousands of examples of how disparate people in our area have come together over the past forty days, utilizing social media for good, instead of harm.

I love scrolling through and seeing the abundance of generosity that is being offered.

Here are some examples of posts I've seen in recent weeks…

"I'm starting a volunteer list here, so we can help neighbors with damaged property. Write your name, availability, and skills below."

"Heads-up: The main highway in ___ section is going to be closed today for reconstruction. Let's help this crew get the work done and not drive that way today."

"Free food today at the ____ Fire Station. All are welcome."

"I have extra clothes, sized X to X. Can anyone use them? I can bring them to you."

"I've got a chainsaw, an ATV, and I'm free all day today. Let me know what you need, and your address."

"Here's a list of resources that are open today for food, water, Wi-Fi, showers, and FEMA."

"Would anyone like my donated Vienna sausages? I'm grateful for them, but I don't personally like them."

Even as people are experiencing their own trauma and devastation, their impetus is to help.

The truth is that we are not wrestling against political beliefs, but against what we stand for as a people.

# Day 36 of the Apocalypse
## Ground Zero, Gerton, NC, Pop. 301

I am not a survivor. To be honest, I've grown to hate that word.

There is no part of me that wants to be known as the person who survived four immediate family members dying by suicide.

Or surviving a 30,000-year geological event that devastated our area. Or surviving rape. Or my childhood. Or whatever.

Surviving suggests that those experiences become the basis from which I operate, make decisions, and function. Surviving keeps me tied to the past. I am not enduring, suffering, or withstanding those experiences.

My spirit is not crushed.

I am not brokenhearted.

Hundreds of condolences for my brother's death have been offered to me. Many people are concerned about my mental well-being. They are imagining themselves in my shoes: weeks with no power, surrounded by devastation, grieving the fourth member of my immediate family to die by suicide.

For many people, all these circumstances would be too much to bear. My not being able to function makes them feel better about their own inability.

I am here for a purpose. When I remember that, everything else comes into sharp perspective.

When you have your consciousness right, you can ride the wave of any situation. If not, you'll find a way to check out. Not everyone is going to make it through the spiritual upgrade that is upon us. The ones who have the best chance know that there is a greater purpose for them.

I've heard this reckoning from many people over the years from the patients I served in a Level 1 hospital who had near-death experiences as well as the locals who survived mudslides or their homes collapsing. Most of them say things like, "God would not have brought me this far to leave me." Or "I knew that God saved me because I have a greater purpose."

Even those of us who did not experience personal catastrophe in the wake of Helene are questioning our purpose. This is part of the spiritual acceleration we are in.

The predictions in Book of Revelation have made themselves manifest, here in the mountains and hollers of Western North Carolina. I don't believe the "end times" means the annihilation of humanity. Rather, there is a reckoning. Who will you become when you have lost everything?

Revelation tells us that the people who can ascend consciousness will stay, not leave. The people who can't evolve will leave. This apocalypse is deconstructing the illusion we have been living in.

This isn't about all of us perishing in the wake of destruction, it's about making the choice to evolve spiritually. Those of us who choose to evolve will stay. We will become the super humans that guide humanity forward.

Restoration is on the other side of loss. Your trauma can become your superpower. My friend Megha reminded me today that "there is equipping even in the greatest of loss." When everything else is ripped from you, your anchors are love and evolution. Fear has no place here.

## The Deep End of Hope in the Wake of Hurricane Helene

I am blessed by an overabundance of possibility. I am blessed by knowing how powerful I am. I am blessed with resiliency. I am blessed by being loved by a power greater than myself.

For me, this is not about getting through. This is about becoming.

Everything that has ever happened, has happened *for* me.

My freedom lies in how I interpret what happens in my reality. My power resides in what I do next, in how I use my skills and gifts in service.

The greatest abundance comes in obeying the path we are called to. The Divine unfolding is that we can't see the path in advance.

The first couple of days after Hurricane Helene hit, it was silent on our mountain. The helicopters hadn't arrived yet. No one had cell service.

Jeff and I sat out in the field next to our house, watching and listening for the smallest indications of life, not yet fully comprehending the devastation below us in the Gorge.

In those forty-eight hours, we made a choice about who we were going to become during this apocalypse.

We decided to become people who made a difference. My role became trauma chaplain. Jeff's role became supply coordinator and chief communicator to the outside world for our community.

These roles have helped us to become this next version of ourselves.

Helping others has allowed us the ability to heal from and process what has happened in our community. It has made us resilient.

My brother dying by suicide showed me what could have happened to me, too, had I not chosen resiliency and strength as my path forward, had I not chosen the path of becoming, instead of surviving.

As humans, we are capable of much more than just enduring. We are designed for miracles. I know that I am miraculous.

You are too.

We are each fully capable of becoming superhuman.

Being superhuman means witnessing immense amounts of suffering, and not taking it on as yours. It means helping others to navigate through it. In the wake of this natural disaster, this is a beacon and an opportunity for all of us to consider our purpose and our work in the world, moving forward.

I hope you choose the path of becoming superhuman.

## Day 37 of the Apocalypse
### Ground Zero, Gerton, NC, Pop. 301

My husband and I do not always see eye-to-eye when it comes to politics. We often vote differently. We often disagree. We have the same fundamental beliefs, but we each have different perspectives about what it will take in order for our nation to support those beliefs.

When we take the time to get into the nitty-gritty of it, we are often surprised by how closely our values align. But on the surface, it can look like they don't.

As a child, I was taught that Conservatives are bad and Liberals are good. It was easy for this belief to be reinforced by my Liberal Quaker community and growing up in Washington, DC. In my childhood, a wild percentage (like 90 percent) of the people who lived in the DC area and worked for the federal government voted Democratic.

I was taught black-and-white thinking, because that is what most of us are taught as children. Categorizing things and people is human nature. Our logical brains can't help but sort things into digestible pieces.

Once, on a whim in my early twenties, I registered as a Republican, just to see what would happen when I went to vote in a primary election near my home in Southwest DC. I was handed a Democratic ticket. The box of Republican tickets hadn't even been opened.

A dozen years ago I moved to North Carolina, a part of the South with a lot of Conservatives. Four years ago, I moved to a teeny tiny community in rural Appalachia full of old-school Conservatives.

I can guess what many of my neighbors 'political views are by whether they were armed during the first weeks of the Apocalypse. But then again, even some Liberals I know were also armed. We have a remarkable diversity of beliefs and values here in our tiny community.

In the wake of the hurricane, we didn't hear anyone talk about politics. For a short time, we lived in a world where politics didn't matter, and it was fucking delightful.

To date, I haven't heard anyone here talk about the presidential election, outside of some rumblings about what Biden, Harris, and Trump did or didn't do in the wake of the hurricane.

"They shouldn't have flown over the devastation."

"They should have flown over the devastation."

"They didn't even try to come see our area."

"They did come to see us, and got in the way by stopping air traffic and emergency work."

"They didn't even donate money for recovery."

"They did donate money, but that was a cop out."

There is always more than one side to a story.

The rules change in the wake of lawlessness. It becomes less about what political beliefs are and more about willingness to step up and do the hard things when the shit hits the proverbial fan.

What might be possible for us as a nation, if instead of choosing division and fear, we all choose to prioritize not only our individual care, but care for our neighbors, regardless of their beliefs or our own?

Political division will not help you when your home is damaged, your power is out, your cell phone has no service, your road is destroyed, and you are running out of food.

It probably would have been easier if I had married someone who always votes the exact same way I do. It would have been easier if I went to church and lived near and was a part of a community of people who always agreed with me. But surrounding myself with people who are different from me has allowed me to grow and evolve as a human. I believe this is my most important work in the world: To keep saying yes. To keep becoming.

There is no us. There is no them.

# Day 38 of the Apocalypse
## Ground Zero, Gerton, NC, Pop. 301

My friend Neal, who lost his home and his income in the wake of Helene, said, "The gift of initiation that this disaster has offered us is to move forward in a more authentic way."

For many of us, that looks like questioning our purpose, in the wake of the hurricane. It looks like stepping more deeply into what brings us joy and satisfaction.

Our friend Brock was over the other night, sharing his deep fulfillment in helping his neighbors by rebuilding roads in the weeks following the hurricane. He's grateful to still have a job but wants to do more. He wants to bring his reconstruction skills back into our community and area, for good. He knows it will take years to rebuild, and this is where his heart is.

Brock isn't alone. A lot of us are thinking the same thing. I mean, not the road-building part, because that takes technical skill. But the intention of aligning our vocations with our hearts.

Our friend Bill came out of retirement as a general contractor because he wants to help people who had their homes damaged.

Jeff thinks this impetus to change and do different work in the world won't last. He heard a lot of people talk this way during Katrina, but then six months later, they were back in their regular jobs. He tends to err on the side of being cynical. I default to optimism.

I hope that all of us continue to evolve as human beings and continue to find ways to give back. I hope that this makes our hearts more tender, our arms more open, and our willingness to do scary things more possible.

For me, following the hurricane and the death of my brothers, I have a whole new life perspective that I'm looking forward to bringing to my work with clients. That's what happens when, in the blink of an eye, you lose what you knew to be true.

My collective trauma hasn't made me want to return to trauma chaplaincy full time or even volunteer in disaster areas. It has caused me to inspire myself and others to play full out in this game called life. Because that's what I'm doing. I'm living for my brothers who died too young. I'm living for my father, who couldn't live for himself. I'm living because I am helping us to evolve as a species.

Many of us are awakening now to our own divinity. In fact, I believe we are going through a major spiritual upheaval. Of course, we each have the choice to evolve spiritually or not. But those of us who chose this path of evolution are in for a magnificent, miraculous ride.

## Day 39 of the Apocalypse
### Ground Zero, Gerton, NC, Pop. 301

Love is what is required to get through this.

Apocalyptic Love is not passive, neither is it always patient or kind. Sometimes it is a fierce warrior in battle or a loud voice, raging. It is a mother bird, protecting her nest.

This Love is giving voice to every person who has lost their home and is being denied coverage by their insurance companies.

This Love is a funeral procession for a person whose body is still missing.

This Love is questioning our president, who did not enact his executive privilege to bring Congress back into session, in order to help the thousands of businesses that have lost everything in the wake of Helene.

This Love is ignoring the red tape, and getting in there and building the road anyway, at your own cost, like miners from West Virginia did last week here in the Hickory Nut Gorge.

This Love is celebrating each small moment of possibility.

This Love is showing up, even when you are too tired, and you have nothing left to give, because your neighbor needs help.

This Love is new, lifelong friendships across political lines.

This Love is burrowing under your covers late into the morning because today you just can't.

This Love is speaking truth to someone else, even when it makes them uncomfortable.

This Love is doing what you need to do, to care for yourself and those around you.

Apocalyptic Love is not always patient and kind. It is an advocating Love, a truthful Love, and a Love that challenges us to find new ways of operating.

# Day 40 of the Apocalypse
## Ground Zero, Gerton, NC, Pop. 301

It is no coincidence that Jeff and I lived in Gerton when Hurricane Helene hit. We were meant to be here.

When I first moved to Asheville a dozen years ago, it was for two reasons. First, God told me to, during a three-day whirlwind visit with a friend about twenty years ago. Second, it was to do residency in a hospital about forty-five minutes south of the city. A year of clinical pastoral education was a requirement for completing seminary and getting my Master of Divinity degree.

The route from my home to the hospital was along the highway that runs through Gerton and straight down the Hickory Nut Gorge. The steep, twisty, two-lane road passes from Gerton through Bat Cave, Chimney Rock, and Lake Lure, and twenty-four miles later eventually lands in Rutherfordton where the hospital was.

At the hospital, I learned that people love to die around me. Every time I would show up for a twenty-four-hour shift someone would pass away. The nurses and doctors began to notice and would flinch when they would see me coming. But I came into my own during that residency. I learned that all the trauma I had experienced in my own life, had uniquely prepared me to attend to others, during their most traumatic moments.

The drive through the Hickory Nut Gorge became my church time. The gorgeous views of the mountains and the sounds of Rocky Broad River rushing alongside the road soothed me. Especially after a twenty-four-hour shift working at the hospital, attending to births, deaths, and everything in between. The Gorge gave me a sense of calm steadiness.

Every time I drove through Gerton I imprinted myself onto the land. Then I started dating a guy, who took me to one of the hiking trails in Gerton on top of a mountain, with 360-degree views of the entire area, and it felt like I had come home.

The relationship with the guy didn't last, but my love for the place did. Now Jeff and I live at the top of that very mountain.

A thousand little decisions over decades brought me to Asheville a dozen years ago, and Jeff to Asheville only a year before we met. While we were dating, I lived just over the continental divide from Gerton, so it was convenient for us to hike the multiple trails in the area.

One day, enroute home from a hike, we noticed that a new business had opened in Gerton: Bearwallow Provision Company. The owners, Erik and Kate, were fifteen to twenty years younger than us, but we felt an immediate kinship with them. Erik and Jeff have almost identical senses of humor and personalities; Kate and I balanced them out. Jeff and I casually mentioned one day that we were looking for property or a house in the area.

About six months later, we stopped by the shop in the middle of the day to grab some beverages after a long, sweaty hike, and to see Erik. He immediately locked eyes with us, asking if we were still in the market for a house. We were. Erik shared that his next-door neighbors, a couple from Florida, were looking to sell. It was a second home for them. One of them had passed the year before, and the other was in her nineties and no longer able to care for two homes.

As Erik was telling us about the house, the caretaker for the home, Bobby, walked into the shop, and offered to take us up the mountain and show us around.

The house was two miles up a steep gravel road. A tiny 1978 yellow cape cod, it was stuffed to the brim with memories and memorabilia, including an inordinate number of plastic, wood, and metal roosters, chickens, and birds. Even the clock hanging on the wall had a cuckoo that would jump out of it at the top of each hour, causing me to recoil. The exterior and interior of the house were the exact opposite of Jeff and me; we both prefer clean, modern design.

But we knew immediately that it was going to be our home. It was as if a lightning bolt went right through both of us when we saw the house and the land. We looked at each other and simultaneously said, "Yes." It's the kind of knowing that runs from the bottom of your toes to the top of your head. Where everything in your body screams "YES!"

Our decision was not a logical one. It was an old house, in an underdeveloped HOA with only eight houses, that was designed to hold seventy-five. It was two miles up a bumpy gravel road, on top of a mountain, and forty minutes from town. We were in the middle of the COVID-19 pandemic, when it was virtually impossible to get building supplies, with up to six-month wait times for everything from lumber to appliances. But we followed our intuition and reached out to the owner that same day. She said yes to our offer.

Due to needing to replace all plumbing, electricity, and walls, we ended up gutting the house down to the studs, keeping only the pine floors, and then doubling the size. We turned it into a black, modern, mountain home. We decided to spend tens of thousands of extra dollars on a whole house generator and a rain catchment system behind our house, to keep water away from our one-level home. These were not things that we had to do to live in the home, but our intuition told us they would be necessary.

After we moved in, we both—especially Jeff—invested time and energy into getting to know our community. Because he is retired, he was able to work at Bearwallow Provision Company one or two days a week to help Erik who was also working as a firefighter. Jeff loved being able to hang out with neighbors, hear the latest gossip, and help tourists navigate our area and hiking trails. Erik, Kate, Jeff, and I began spending even more time together because our homes were next to each other.

Jeff and I will always be considered outsiders, because our last names are foreign here, and because we have not lived here for generations. Our family name is not on a street sign. It doesn't matter how involved we were in our community, following the wake of Helene, there will always be the reminder that we are not *from* here. We still claim this place we do not belong to as our forever home. This is the place that has defined who we are becoming.

None of what unfolded in our journey to living on top of our favorite mountain, in the middle of Gerton, was a coincidence. It was all preordained.

A thousand little decisions and coincidences brought us to this particular place, at this particular time, with these particular people, so that when Helene hit, we could be here to help.

# Reflections on Trauma in the Evolution Phase

We become what we focus on. In the evolution phase of trauma, our work becomes holding our focus on what we most desire in the midst of chaos.

Approximately a gazillion times a day, I remind myself that things are all going to work out. That the entire world of insurance companies and governmental institutions is full of people who want to help. New trees will grow. Roads and homes will be rebuilt. Our hearts will not always ache. We are not alone in this.

The devastation will eventually be transformed. I am already transforming.

And that Helene happened *for* me, not *to* me.

I am able to move from anger, frustration, and sadness into acceptance when I stay present in the moment with what is true.

I am still safe.

I am still warm.

I am still fed.

I am still loved.

I am still able to care for myself and others.

My life has become moments of just doing the next thing right in front of me. Feed the dogs. Check email. Make a phone call. Move my body. Check on the people I love. Breathe. Eat. Sleep.

Chop the wood. Carry the water. Show up and attend to what is needed.

It is easy to self-manage emotions, decisions, and actions in times of peace, and in solitude. But how do you do this in the midst of chaos, confusion, tension, and pressure? That is our real work as humans.

We must learn to process our trauma as we are living in it. As we are moving through it. As we are transforming it. It's all happening, simultaneously, in real time. This is the brave new world we are already living in.

In the evolution phase, we are becoming the people who can live in *and* process trauma simultaneously. Healing doesn't stop with the relieving of pain. It continues beyond that, in our search for Love. Love is the gateway to our evolution as humans and is how we process as we go.

Love what is. Love yourself in this moment. Love the person who tells you no, after you've already heard no ten times over. Love every person who has helped. Love the land for its capacity to heal. Love your home for what it was and what it can become. Love your neighbors when they are doing their best. Love all of the people who will never understand this devastation. Love being alive at this particular time, in this particular moment. Love who you are becoming.

In the wake of Helene there is a Love that will not let us go. Gratitude becomes our weapon of warfare. Presence is our battlefield. Focus is our battle plan.

This is a fierce Love.

The highest potential expression of humanity is rooted in Love. It is time for us to rise to this expression as a species, to save ourselves.

A prayer/poem I wrote during a time of great evolution, personally:

## The Deep End of Hope in the Wake of Hurricane Helene

In that space

where the stars disappear

In that space

where water covers the earth

and lightning strikes down

and clouds rail above

Offer up a blessing

for eternity

Offer up a blessing

for your children's children's children

Offer up a blessing

for the revolution

for we are on a pilgrimage towards Love

We are on a pilgrimage

towards faith

towards truth

towards surrender

We have already begun

Friends!

We have already begun

# EPILOGUE

It has been forty days and forty nights since Hurricane Helene devastated Western North Carolina and other parts of the Southeast.

There are many stories I was unable to capture in this book. Stories from members of our own community, as well as from other parts of North Carolina, and the Southeast. All of these stories deserve to be told too.

This book is by no means an historical account of what happened. It is my small recollection, in the midst of a traumatizing event, where on some days I couldn't get my brain to work enough to use the internet or remember to eat. It is a slightly accurate account of some things that happened to a group of people who were doing the best they could during a horrendous time.

I wrote the majority of this book in forty days, on the Notes app of my phone and while hanging out at the fire station or in the middle of the night, when I couldn't sleep. I interviewed people and attempted to capture their perspectives. In quiet moments, I tried to understand and share my own perspective, too. There are many firsthand accounts included in the book, but they by no means tell the whole story. There is much more to understand about the impact of this tremendous event.

Hurricane Helene was a 30,000-year storm event. This was the most catastrophic tropical storm event that has happened on our continent, according to NOAA data. The hurricane ravaged parts of North and South Carolina, Florida, Georgia, Tennessee, and Virginia.

As of November 1, 2024, at least 230 people have been declared dead, according to NBC News. Nearly half, 102, of those fatalities were here in North Carolina. Helene is the deadliest hurricane to strike US mainland since Katrina in 2005. CBS news called this biblical devastation.

That phrase, *biblical devastation*, hit me like a sucker punch. That is exactly what our reality feels like. This is the type of devastation that belongs in the Bible.

I am not downplaying or dismissing any other devastation that has happened on our planet. I am saying that since September 26th, our reality has changed forever. What happened to us is unprecedented.

I am a different person than I was forty days ago. There is no normal to return to. There isn't a new normal, either. We are living in a liminal never-never land where the future can't even be considered, because we are still in the middle of the action.

Last night we had freezing temperatures here in the mountains. People whose houses were destroyed are living in tents without heat. Over two thousand households are still without power. Thousands continue to live without potable water.

The destruction will take years to rebuild.

Media attention for this event has already died down. Volunteer support has already slowed.

We are only forty days into this event, and people are already forgetting.

---

A portion of the proceeds from this book will go to Mennonite Disaster Service. They were one of the first groups to make it to Gerton and offered invaluable assistance in clearing trees off of homes.

*Mennonite Disaster Service is a volunteer network through which various groups within the Anabaptist tradition assist people affected by disasters in North America. The organization was founded in 1950 and was incorporated as a 501(c)(3) nonprofit organization in 1993.*

# NEXT STEPS

# Your Next Steps

There are four ways to continue this important work of trauma recovery immediately:

1. **Leave a book review** wherever you bought this book to let others know how it impacted you. Very few people are talking about how to process trauma as they are going through it. Please help spread this important message.

2. **Enroll in my online course**, Trauma Recovery in Real Time, for additional support with your personal situation (learn more on the following pages).

3. **Invite me to speak** to your community, organization, corporation or at an event about how to process trauma as you are going through it (learn more on the following pages).

4. **Email me personally** to let me know how this book impacted you at emma@emmachurchman.com. I'd love to hear from you.

Love,

Emma

# Trauma Recovery in Real Time
# Self-led Online Course

No one delights in living with trauma. The anxiety, brain fog, sleeplessness, exhaustion, and frustration are not ways of being that anyone aspires to.

We want relief from these symptoms, and we want it now. We don't want to spend years in the future, reliving everything that happened to us, in search of relief.

Gone are the days of lying on a therapist's couch, slowly working through our feelings. We do not have that luxury of time anymore.

The world is speeding up, and so is our need to process trauma as we are going through it. That is what the COVID-19 pandemic taught all of us and is what a disaster or unexpected event or challenge will show you, too.

It is possible to avoid suffering the long-term effects of trauma. It is possible to not just get through life but to actually thrive in it. I want to show you how to accelerate your healing and recovery.

That's why I created **Trauma Recovery in Real Time: Four Weeks to Freedom from Overwhelm.**

In this course I will show you how to address the physical, emotional, mental, and spiritual aspects of trauma so that your body, mind, and spirit can quickly transform horrendous side effects and symptoms into a new way of living. No special skills are required, and you can benefit from this course whether you consider yourself spiritual, religious, or not.

This **self-led online course**, with daily guidance from me, only requires **fifteen minutes a day**. With a combination of video teachings and exercises, the course is very easy to follow and won't feel like one more thing you just have to "get through." At the end of each day's fifteen-minute activity, you will notice an immediate difference.

By the end of the course, you will shift from feeling like everything is too much to trusting yourself to be able to function well.

The course is available to you as soon as you enroll.

When you enroll, you're also given an incredible **bonus opportunity** to join me on a **monthly group Q+A call**, where I answer your questions and offer personalized guidance for working through trauma in real time.

Learn more and enroll:

emmachurchman.com/trauma

# Keynote Speaker

Emma Churchman is a spiritual and business leader with over 25 years of experience helping thousands transform trauma into hope and strength. Drawing from her own journey of overcoming childhood adversity, Emma's work as a trauma chaplain and mentor inspires resilience.

Her book, *The Deep End of Hope in the Wake of Hurricane Helene*, explores spiritual strength during disaster recovery. As a sought-after speaker and PhD candidate in Conscious Business Ethics, Emma combines soulful leadership with actionable strategies, all from her mountaintop home in Gerton, North Carolina, shared with her husband and two dachshunds.

**Why Emma's Story Matters:**

- **Timely and Universal Topics:** Leadership during disasters, spiritual resilience, and real-time trauma recovery.
- **Inspiring Personal Journey:** Emma's triumph over her own trauma adds authenticity and depth to her message.
- **Practical Takeaways:** Actionable steps for individuals and businesses to navigate and prepare for traumatic events.

**Speaking Highlights and Topics:**

1. **The Role of a Trauma Chaplain:** Why spiritual support is critical in disaster response.
2. **Practical Strategies:** How businesses can prepare for and recover from catastrophic events.
3. **Everyday Resilience:** Steps anyone can take to better prepare for unexpected crises.
4. **Behind the Book:** Insights into *The Deep End of Hope in the Wake of Hurricane Helene* and a sneak peek at her next book, releasing in 2025.

To inquire about Emma speaking to your community, organization, corporation, or at an event about how to process trauma as you are going through it

email: support@emmachurchman.com
or go to

emmachurchman.com/speaking

# ACKNOWLEDGMENTS

Thank you to the people of Gerton, North Carolina, for allowing me to walk beside you during this strange time.

To my husband, Jeff Boudreaux: Thank you for being my biggest supporter and for being eternally brave, especially during moments I can't be and for loving me through the most challenging of times. You will always be my favorite husband.

To our neighbors, Erik Julian and Kate Loughran: You are the people I most want to live next to during an apocalypse. Thank you for your friendship and support.

To members of our community, including Fire Chief Jay Alley and his wife Carolyn, Assistant Chief Norris Lyda, Firefighters Jacob Lyda and Jamie White, Dave MacDonald, Julia Pierce, DJ Steele, Graham Sturgis, our close neighbors on the mountain, and everyone else who I mentioned in this book: Thank you for trusting me to carry your stories forward and for your support when I needed it.

To all of the people who agreed to be interviewed in Gerton and Bat Cave, especially Rich Coggins, firefighter Jenn White, and those who wished to remain anonymous, thank you.

To those who donated to our area, or who showed up and volunteered, thank you for your service.

To my clients, thank you for understanding when I needed time and space to attend to myself and my community during the fall of 2024.

To all of those who followed my story on Facebook and sent love and encouragement, and to everyone who prayed for me and for Gerton: We heard your prayers. I felt your prayers.

Thank you to *The Guardian* and journalist Rachel Obordo, for publishing my first story about Hurricane Helene in October 2024.

To GracePoint Publishing and Michelle Vandepas, thank you for giving me the opportunity to publish this story.

To all of those who encouraged me and helped me to develop aspects of this book, including Megha Bradley, Peggy Diggs, Ed Epping, Mark Etheridge, and Angie Stegall: I am deeply grateful.

To all those who continue to live in the wake of Hurricane Helene: I see you and I believe in you.

# ABOUT THE AUTHOR

**Emma M. Churchman, M.Div**

**Speaker, Author, Mentor, and Spiritual Advisor**

Emma Churchman is a beacon of resilience and transformation. With over 25 years of experience as a spiritual and business leader, Emma has guided thousands through the labyrinth of trauma to reclaim hope and strength. Her powerful work as a trauma chaplain and mentor is rooted in her own journey of overcoming acute childhood adversity.

Her book, *The Deep End of Hope in the Wake of Hurricane Helene*, takes readers on an unforgettable journey of spiritual resilience during one of nature's most catastrophic events. Emma is a sought-after speaker and coach, teaching trauma recovery techniques that empower individuals and organizations alike.

As a PhD candidate in Conscious Business Ethics, Emma bridges the gap between soulful leadership and practical strategies for navigating life's storms. From the picturesque mountain peaks of Gerton, North Carolina, where she lives with her husband Jeff and their dachshunds Winston and Leroy, Emma inspires people to find strength even in the darkest of times.

For more great books from Empower Press
Visit Books.GracePointPublishing.com

If you enjoyed reading *The Deep End of Hope in the Wake of Hurricane Helene* and purchased it through an online retailer, please return to the site and write a review to help others find the book.